MW00668297

The Thoughtful Gardener

Jinny Blom

The Thoughtful Gardener

Jinny Blom

Dedicated with love to Marc Fox

First published in 2017 by
Jacqui Small LLP
The Old Brewery, 6 Blundell Street
London, N7 9BH
Text, garden plans and sketches copyright
© 2017 by Jinny Blom
Design and layout copyright
© 2017 Jacqui Small LLP

All gardens illustrated are designed
by Jinny Blom.

The author's moral rights have been asserted.

All rights reserved. No part of this book
may be reproduced, stored in a retrieval
system or transmitted, in any form or by any
means, electronic, electrostatic, magnetic
tape, mechanical, photocopying, recording or
otherwise, without prior permission in writing
from the publisher.

Publisher: Jacqui Small
Senior Commissioning Editor: Eszter Karpati
Managing Editor: Emma Heyworth-Dunn
Designer: Mark Paton
Editor: Sian Parkhouse
Production: Maeve Healy

ISBN: 9781910254592
A catalogue record for this book is available
from the British Library.

2020
10 9

Printed in China

PAGE 1 A tendril of the annual *Cobaea scandens* bathed
in soft summer sun.

PAGES 2–3 Abundant and unfettered planting layers
gently up from *Viola cornuta* Alba Group through the
rose garden with its topiary cones. These lead into
carefully planned boundary hedges marrying the
woodland beyond.

THIS PAGE Choosing how to end the garden was easy.
Estate railing and a sweep of beautifully managed floral
grassland were sufficient.

Contents

Foreword

The loose informality of planting below the *Rosa glauca* all but hides the sturdy oak gate in the old wall (OPPOSITE). Softly clipped *Quercus ilex* draw the eye and suggest there is more to discover.

Rare is the garden book, like this one, that makes the reader feel personally included as a friend in a long conversation with the writer. We set out with the author Jinny Blom as she interweaves early family experiences, including childhood visits to Hidcote Manor and an uncle's vineyard in France, and moves inextricably, though unexpectedly at first, to a full-blown life as a landscape designer on an international scale. Her education evolves from the worlds of literature and the arts, as well as previous work as a psychologist, and frequent references say to Thomas Hardy or Cy Twombly and others reveal the breadth of her intrinsic knowledge.

Like Lancelot 'Capability' Brown, whom she lauds for his estate management in the 18th century, Blom is herself a cultural geographer who scopes out the historical features of paths, gates and antiquated farm buildings on a given property prior to drawing up a plan that proceeds almost instantaneously, a process fascinating to follow. Whether in town or country, with either single or multiple garden areas, Blom establishes architectural enclosures, like Cotswold drystone walls, prior to the overlay of her signature, beautifying horticulture, thus creating what she calls 'environments for intimate experiences'.

In the end, Blom radiates a humanistic approach to landscape design, combining her fascination with physical traces from former lives with her ultimate concern for present owners and the transforming effects of gardens. While she subscribes to traditional features like topiary, pleaching and espaliered fruit trees, and stitches together native plants with other ornamental species and grasses with year-round interest, her romantic borders possess a contained but natural simplicity that speaks of modernity. By generously sharing her theories, and teaching us how to read the land, Blom has set forth an unforgettable, sui generis narrative that thankfully demonstrates that she is, in her own words, 'unmoved by fashion'.

Paula Deitz
Editor, *The Hudson Review*

Waking up
How it all began

Why am I writing a book?

    The route of my life has always unfolded as I walked. I wasn't born with a clear path before me. I had my anagnorisis, my critical discovery about myself, at the age of 36 when I was comfortably ensconced in a career I loved. I use the term deliberately, because if you choose to follow an uncharted path, then the outcome is far from certain.

    I was on holiday in northern Spain, in the Picos de Europa. The Picos Mountains are very inaccessible and remote, or at least they were, and are best navigated on foot. Each day I set off up a mountain track alone. Sitting on a rocky outcrop to rest one day I watched two old men on the other side of the steep narrow valley making hay. They scythed the small, near vertical meadow in easy strokes from one side to the other, rolling the resulting neat cylinder of hay downhill before them. I was mesmerized by the process. At the bottom of the meadow a silent donkey stood tethered to a tiny high-sided cart made of ash wands bound together with leather straps. The men finally hoisted their sausage rolls into the cart and off they went. The scythe marks left on the scalped meadow were beautiful, like fish scales in a child's drawing. I watched the empty meadow a while more and set off. Along the path I encountered beautiful plants scattered here and there. There were exquisite hellebores with tiny flowers, *Helleborus viridis* subsp. *occidentalis* to be precise. They had a character all of their own up here in the rocks. A little further on were pinging electric blue eryngiums. I made a note in my pocket book and hunted around for seed. They were so attractive and far surpassed any wild flowers I'd seen in England.

It is very freeing to remove erroneous things and feel the essential character of a place sing out. I strive for the clarity it brings.

    I was mulling about the hay meadow almost constantly during my walks and came across one that was uncut. It was absolutely crammed with different species and not very many of them were grass. Finding some suitable sticks, I marked out a square meter or so and started to count what I found in it. It amazed me. There were over a hundred species. I've always been captivated by plants and have a fascination for wild plants and their uses, so this was deeply absorbing and many hours flew by. As I walked on I thought about domestic herbivores — if they lived on a diet of this hay, they would be ingesting a banquet of herbs every day. Their milk would be incredible, filled with flavour and health. The term 'herbivore' took on a refreshed meaning. In appalling Spanish I'd spoken to an old woman in the local market who explained that until very recently the Picos had been almost entirely cut off from the rest of Spain

This is my London garden the first time I consciously designed it in around 1997 (BELOW). I always loved the infinity view to the woods and hilltops beyond – not a building to be seen. A very fine wispy mix of planting makes it feel diffuse, delicate and soft. I wanted the garden to blend into the natural surroundings and make it feel remote from the centre of a heaving metropolis that is only 40m (44 yards) away. This little garden defined something for me and I've been developing it ever since.

as it is accessed through a difficult gorge. She said that they hardly used money, had no electricity and lived by bartering food and materials. They had everything they needed.

For days I walked and walked, lost in thought. As I rounded a corner I snapped awake. In front of me, below a hazel, was a clump of *Digitalis parviflora*, the little brown-flowered foxglove. I was stunned and excited. Unbelievably excited! I'd never seen it in the wild before, only in books.

That night I had a vivid dream. I was in a crowded football stadium filled with screaming fans. Beside me a small child I didn't know was trying to get my attention. He was insistent and inaudible. Eventually I bellowed out into the stadium: 'Will you all please be quiet – the child wants to say something.' Silence. I bent down and he whispered: 'Please may I be a gardener?' It might sound daft but that was that.

Returning home I went back to my job but something was stirring that I couldn't still. Always obsessed with plants I was now on fire with them. The eryngium I'd found, naturally convinced I was the only person to have ever seen it, turned out to be on sale through the Royal Horticultural Society as *Eryngium bourgatii* 'Picos Blue'!

Over the next couple of months a great rumble of events took place, supported and provoked by good friends. Specifically, I was spending a lot of time with John Harris OBE and his wife Dr Eileen Harris, architectural

scholars, historians and landscape historians, and Eileen a great gardener. With John and Eileen constantly telling me I should be gardening, I felt it rude to gainsay them! Protesting that I couldn't give up my 'sensible' job as a psychologist, I found I couldn't make an argument for keeping it. Having resigned my post, I began designing gardens two days later. It was a leap of faith, literally, and not just for me but also for my early clients who now laugh with me about my shy earnestness.

I was very conscious of my deficiencies. I did know a prodigious amount of Latin names of plants, but I'd never really tested that knowledge in planting anything other than my own garden. I also had an enthusiasm for architecture and practical building. And from my prior work I could sniff people out quite well, add up with the aid of a calculator and file things neatly. What more could I possibly need? How hard could it be? It was up to me to learn, research my subject, think before I act and not let anyone down. I'd been brought up to ask questions and be honest about what I did and didn't know. Armed with energy, enthusiasm and blind faith, I got going. I had become an apprentice.

So this book is about how I've developed my way of working over the last twenty years in my progression from apprentice to journeyman to master craftsman. I have always felt it necessary to 'learn the trade' properly. It takes a long time and I've learned at the elbow of countless masters, not in a schoolroom. I have been helped, encouraged and inspired by lots of people along the way. Whatever I've absorbed has been freely taught and this book and my working life are underpinned by the generosity of those erudite souls I've encountered.

It seems blindingly obvious now, and is certainly on everyone's lips these days, but probably the most valuable insight from the Picos de Europa was that things that work together in natural harmony are beautiful. I choose plants with compatibility in mind, appropriate materials arise from their locale, and I consider the people who will live in the garden, the wildlife, the weather. I'd like to share some of what I think about when designing, in the hope that it kindles the fires of excitement in others.

I've climbed a big mountain to get to this point and hope there's a view worth sharing.

We depend on ourselves for our happiness so following a creative urge is essential to that happiness.

An early morning in early spring in the foggy gorge where I live in France (OPPOSITE). I find great inspiration in how effortlessly plants cohabit in nature. The mosses are steadily eating the clay-tiled roof of the timeworn shed and the quince embracing it while, in turn, being woven through with eglantine roses. The layering of the grasses and mints in the ditch makes this a very painterly scene.

Seeing

Seeing is not just about the gift of sight, it is about the dawning of greater comprehension and deeper insight into a subject. Gardening is a profound holistic experience. All our responses quicken when outside. Our sophisticated minds are alive not just to our physical surroundings, but to many levels of information fed into us through brains capable of sorting instinct, emotion and reason. Humans are unique in being able to ingest information from the world around them and process it, reforming and replaying it to create culture. *It is the 'duende' of music and art.* The 'soul' is often referred to in things that move us. It is a life-bringing, glittering instinctive understanding that something is beautiful.

Trusting your instincts

Understanding how to make a space flow and be pleasant comes to me very quickly. It's a knack I've always had. More often than not when I arrive somewhere new I get to grips with what needs altering within hours. It's a sort of fact-based intuition. Having a little knowledge of many things allows for a shorthand in comprehension. I always try to check this instinctive understanding factually, though, as it could be precarious to rely on it.

When I first started out in garden design I had a fear of making obvious mistakes. To manage the anxiety I used to employ what I'd learned during my experiences in stage design at drama college. We were shown how actors expressed emotion physically in gesture and then how to create a physical space that allowed them to do it unconsciously. It was absolutely invaluable. So from early on I would peg out spaces on site and walk around in them, feeling the comfort of the enclosure I was imagining. The dynamics of passing through a garden are fascinating, so the cadence of moving from room to room needs to be examined and understood in this way. In the early days I'd rig gardens up in canes and string to get the wall heights and meterage of the room. Steps and stairs are particularly challenging to get right, and the riser height and length of stride, especially uphill, are best learned in this way. Calculations from books are only standards, not nuanced to a place, so I developed the skill through action. I still do it like this now, judging by the sticks all over the garden!

I believe fear should always be present when designing, as only when this heightened state starts to calm down do you understand that a good design is within grasp. I work out every level and every dimension on plan, of course, but then I invariably want to test it. Thankfully these terms are now within my lexicon, but they are not always within that of my patrons, so the mock-up is alive and well and we frequently peg out so that they can walk around the imagined space.

Landscape designing is never dull. Restructuring the physical land to meet the aspirations of a commission is just a facet of it. Light, seasons, climate, time, architecture, growth, decay, function, history, culture, decoration, nature and beauty are all there to be considered. That is a lot of moving parts to blend into a unified whole. It is a prodigious act of creation. It reminds me of the alchemic process of 'solutio' that I learned about during my years of Jungian training. The alchemists thought that a substance could not be transformed unless it were first reduced to its 'prima materia', and this I feel is somehow

The garden planting blends effortlessly into the natural surroundings of the Cotswolds. (PREVIOUS PAGES). Using fruit trees and keeping them tightly pruned maintains everything in scale. The planting becomes simpler the closer to the field gate we get — foxgloves, valerian and semi-wild roses.

I strongly believe that outside spaces cannot be designed in CAD. Computers undeniably have a place and we all use them, but a genuine appreciation of the emotional and esoteric aspects of design can only be understood if one actually gets to grips with how the space feels.

This is a seminal view for me (BELOW). I think all my gardening thoughts were generated from seeing medieval villages in France hugging rocks and embedded in native planting. The roofs peeking above the wild oak trees and the punctuation of a few non-native thuja among the buildings are the discreet indicators of human activity. In the village the streets billow with lilacs, quinces and honeysuckle.

what is required for good landscaping — washing through the subject 'in solutio' again and again to find the essence of what is really desirable and discarding all that seems dross. Ultimately my design layouts become quite unassuming. I'm a great 'reductionista!

The simplicity of a few carefully considered lines on paper amounts to my sense of beauty. The lines can be pure and clear, as there are still so many aspects of the garden to come. For example, the volatility of light, the weather and planting lend their own layers of grace. There is a wonderful moment in designing when the muddy waters swirling around in my mind go clear and I can see what I'm doing. It hasn't got much to do with picking a specific style, as my tastes are varied and eclectic. It's very hard to describe what happens when I think I've nailed a design. It's almost physical — something goes 'clunk' and the process concludes. All the whirring cogs stop. These days I just think it's a sort of natural process I've honed over time. I never studied this subject, so it's not been acquired academically. I trained myself and learned through asking endless questions of good-natured collaborators like my friend Robert Crocker, who has built many gardens for me. I am indebted to this generosity.

Almost every style of architecture and design offers me things to appreciate. I enjoy the challenge of studying to understand something that initially jars. There is satisfaction in learning enough of a new subject's specific, coded language to allow access to its mystery. Once I grasp the essence of what is being expressed, it opens new doors of perception and that makes my working life a very satisfying one.

Time is another dimension that is so essential to this work. In garden-making it is vital to hold the long view. Although I'll never live long enough to see them, the future growth of trees and hedges is vital to the larger picture. The weathering of materials, the true pattern and purpose of routes and pathways, are all in my hands at the outset, yet will develop their character over time. In my village in France I'm very aware that the tracks are ancient and, considering the relatively inhospitable topography, find comfort that the well-trodden path exists. The landscapes I create are newborn and I must leave them early, trusting time to take the original layout and romance it. That's what I see when I arrive at a new place: initially the discomfort and ultimately the beauty, romance and freedom.

The thatched classical temple is by architect Charles Morris and terminates one of the serpentine shrubberies at The Menagerie (BELOW). Planting was a complete trial on the heavy waterlogged clay, yet mountains of sand and perseverance improved matters over time. Thank goodness for *Geranium phaeum* 'Album'!

This epitomizes French insouciance, translating as 'a casual lack of concern' (OPPOSITE). The Virginia creeper is allowed to grow through the pot and at the same time is meticulously pruned every year. *Acanthus mollis* and a nameless *Iris germanica* coexist peacefully and indestructibly in the driest of dry places at the base of the house. My kind of garden.

Understanding

Taking the pulse of the land is vital to my approach to designing. Before starting any drawings a good chunk of *information needs gathering together*. Get out there and sniff the air. Bury your nose in books and maps and uncover the local history. Consider the weather patterns and microclimates. Prowl around the fields and lanes or streets and see what's growing, what other people are growing and what the views are like. Understand what drew you to the place – it must have been something special that you fell for. And what are your aspirations? Let's gather the raw ingredients required for creating the new Elysian fields.

Respecting what you unearth

I'm a natural enthusiast and get incredibly excited about new projects. From the initial meeting I become a sponge for all the information that is about to come to light.

The exploration of the subject starts long before you actually arrive on site. I enjoy deciphering a landscape. I love geography and geology, and it does help to give thought to the nature of the land you are about to alter. How did it come to be the way it is, what actually happened, prehistorically, to the earth? What have been the ancient and traditional movements of people across the land? The better the understanding of it at the start, the more likely the end result is to turn out well. I live in England, one of the most diverse landscapes on earth in relation to its size. As an old country it has seen many levels of conditioning by its past through architecture and human activity and these are still visible if you are able to tune your eyes. I can decipher quite a lot just by looking, common sense combining with a degree of knowledge.

It is very easy to make assumptions about land and I'm frequently surprised, when I dig a little deeper, that the character and historic usage were radically different from the vestiges we see today. One project I had was set on the edge of what I assumed were naturally occurring beech forests. Reading up on the history of the area unearthed the surprising discovery that these forests were largely man-made. The original forests had been an appealing mixture of oak, cherry, holly and ash. The beech had been planted in huge quantity to support the local chair-making industry — now long defunct. Back in the 1700s the beech would have been managed on coppice rotations and the indigenous oak forest strategically felled and sold for shipbuilding or construction. This intense yet natural use of the land slowly altered the character of the landscape as the forest species changed. The area is nowadays justly famed for its beautiful beech and bluebell woods, and we take them completely for granted as 'natural'.

Slowing back down to walking pace is also really useful when considering the scale of relationship between a new garden and an existing landscape. I have a near-medieval inclination towards manual labour, and land-workers deal with the details of the natural world at a human pace. This pace dictates comfortable spacing between trees, heights of walls and distances between buildings. It is why we love old villages and settlements: they have a proportion born of humanity and kindred relationships. I like to delve deeply into the

This is a created view (OPPOSITE). I cleared lots of Victorian tree planting that blocked the view to the water and included a wellingtonia over 36m (120 feet) tall. I stripped away mature Leyland cypress on the right-hand side, replaced them with a native hedge and created a ha-ha from where this image is taken. The view to the tiny Windrush River flowing through the wild irises and the medieval mill pond is now restored.

We inherited a few magnificent old field trees here (PREVIOUS PAGES) and I wanted to blend the gardens out towards the fields and create a solid visual relationship between new and old. We have planted an ornamental 'mead' filled with tulips and alliums, their seed heads just visible in the sheets of poppies and cornflowers.

Landscapes last a long time if they are done well, so honouring them with a bit of thought at the start stabilizes the design process.

landscape and the architecture, draw out its beauty and compliance and then integrate it back into the design work. This way it is easy to create places that suit their location, rather than rubberstamping a sole identity onto everything one touches.

For me it is about respecting the place I find myself in, and trying not to be too cocky about my big ideas before I've really had time to submerge myself in the area. For example, the profundity of things I've discovered about one of my new garden projects has stopped me dead in my tracks. I learned it is built over the long-lost ruins of an historic palace of national significance. We are now undertaking serious research into the recent past as well as the local geology and archaeology, and are discovering things that are making the design work so much richer. With the discoveries also come enriching stories that will help to make the new gardens captivating long into the future.

Wild roses abound in local field hedges and in autumn their magnificent hips gradually turn a rich scarlet, creating sparks of colour (LEFT). I've always found them beautiful and plant them freely on wild margins. Their hips contain a lot of vitamin C and were extensively used during World War II to create syrup for children.

As the garden bleeds out towards nature I wanted to create a visual relationship with the wild roses in the outlying hedgerows. This is a great cascading bank of *Rosa californica* 'Plena' (OPPOSITE). A trouble-free, single-flowering semi-double and exquisitely scented rose, it is redolent of summer and massed with orange hips in autumn. Quite a sight.

Geology
The structure of the countryside

What is the structure of the countryside? What is the underlying physical nature of the land? These questions set up an investigation that will allow the resulting garden to be properly and pleasingly related to its environment.

A glaciated landscape, for example, moulded and scoured by slow-moving ice floes into distinctive U-shaped valleys, is very obvious to see once your eye acclimatizes to it. In tandem with past glacial movement come readily understandable paths of water in the valley bottoms and down the steep hillsides. This water runs in fast spating streams, pitching down the steep valley sides into rivers flowing over the remnant glacial moraine of rolled rock and gravel with its distinctive rounded shape.

The shape of the land implicates its function. Valleys tend to be fertile, but this fertile land is limited, so there might be grazing cattle here where grass can grow. But the associated high rainfall and cool conditions indicate short seasons for crops, so arable farming is generally less viable. The steep rocky valley sides might be useful for grazing sheep but the inevitable high rainfall leeches nutrients and leaves soil that is thin, acidic and relatively infertile. Grass growth is weaker, yet in turn this allows more wildflower activity. So, historically, how else could people sustain themselves here other than keeping a low population density? Quarrying, of course. How are the houses built? Stone: slate for roofing, granite for building and limestone for steelmaking. By assessing the local architecture one immediately has the locally appropriate lexicon for building a new landscape.

My experience working on the volcanic east coast of Scotland, and my French experience in the Auvergne, helped me work in Kenya in the Rift Valley. I could tell that the Kenyan landscape was volcanic simply by its shape and colour and by the rock debris that is typical of expulsive volcanic activity. To be fair, it's a pretty obvious call as Mount Kenya looks like a volcano as it rises to its conical peak. The land is dry red and dusty and covered in rough low grasses that bind it. All around are gobbets of black rock shaded with the orange rusting of iron ore and with the peculiarly smooth finish of something once malleable that hurtled through the air and cooled as it flew. There are also smaller bits of aerated pumice that would

In the recent past, houses were built using stone from small localized quarries. Sufficient stone for building would be blasted and the resulting crater left to naturalize. These are easy to find if you look for them.

The mountainous limestone outcrops at home in France allow tiny gardens of box and helianthemum to manifest in the crevices (OPPOSITE). The plants are bonsai'd by their location and take on forms that suit the circumstances. Lower down in the fertile valley the same box grows to a forest.

From the unmade road on the approach to a project in Scotland it is clear to see this is a classic U-shaped glacial valley, scoured and shaped by creaking ice floes (ABOVE). The absence of trees is man-made. They will grow even at this altitude, and occasionally a downy birch is visible in the crags.

have been flung from the volcano over two million years ago and still litter the ground today. The structural stone for the house we were building was mined from one of these pumice seams — it can be sawn by hand and is very light and is, effectively, blockwork. I also used it crushed up into gravel on the green roofs to create a base reservoir, as it has the capacity to hold a lot of water and release it slowly.

I'm always amazed at the complementary qualities of natural materials — here in such a dry place, with only two episodes of annual rainfall, to have a material that acts like an oasis is a perfect symbiosis. This same 'tufo' is found in Italy and is used extensively in the decorative rustication of gardens such as the Villa d'Este. I love it, as when it is constantly saturated by cool fresh dripping water, it creates a micro world of mosses and ferns and is a beautiful adjunct in a blisteringly hot country.

The plant matrix
Demeanour of the countryside

I have found that once I understand the physical structure of the ground it doesn't really matter which country I am in as, functionally, it behaves in a way I can recognize and work with. It is then quick and enjoyable work to get to grips with the plant species that will thrive and to create a palette of ingredients for that place. Wherever it is on earth I am now confident in my approach to unravelling the story of the place and with it the nature of the project. I like plants to live out long happy lives. A diet of native plants alone makes a dull garden, and I would not advocate it. However, I might thread native species through ornamentals if it adds authenticity to a place. It really depends on how much space there is and the desired result.

In a project in New York State I needed to find a way to fuse the new gardens into an exceedingly rugged wild environment. In the recent past the substantial houses of the area had simply set up strict boundaries around their gardens and kept nature out and ornamental planting in. These gardens are very much of their time, and the ornamental plants are cosseted and coaxed to live in an environment they fundamentally detest. I went for more warp and weft of the natural and the ornamental, and stitched a very carefully curated list of plants in and out of the garden and native surroundings. The result can naturalize easily and still has a designed integrity that is discernible. This sort of planting is not without its perils, and it is extremely important to ensure that ornamentals are not going to escape into the wild and cause havoc.

In a city garden the choice of planting is much more to do with microclimate and the effects of surrounding buildings than with geology. Generally the evolution of a city will have denaturized a garden to an extreme degree – in some cases even the soil isn't original. One garden I made in town started with the need to block out everything on its boundaries. I was asked if I could re-create the 'limitless veldt' of my client's South African childhood. We both laughed out loud, as the garden was only 12m (40 feet) deep, but it did give a very good basis for the planting matrix. I chose lots of compatible South African and antipodean species and wove them into a pleasingly rugged scheme. We altered the soil appropriately, adding grit and pumice to keep it free draining. We craned in some vast contorted cryptomeria and pine, and *voilà*! Suddenly we had an evocation of a purely imaginary landscape.

Choosing the plants for this New York City garden was easy, as they needed to replicate the shrubby woodland floor (ABOVE). In this part of the city the villas were built into the indigenous woodland, and the forest glade feel is very chic and relaxing.

I often sketch accurate scaled sections in order to think through the proportions of trees I'm proposing (OPPOSITE). It is a waste of life to plant the wrong thing only to have to take it away in a few years. The Sitka spruce in the background was an introduced species from the forestry commission and is almost a pernicious weed. In the foreground is a stretch of lochside that we cleared and returned to the softer deciduous indigenous species, and the 'hairy' sauna lodge blends in.

Studying old maps
Links and relationships

The masterplan design of several of my larger projects in the UK has come about directly as the result of historic research. I'm a bit of a map enthusiast, which is a helpful trait in this line of work. It is fascinating to be able to look back in time on an old map and see how the roads used to run and where buildings once stood.

The new structural layout of Temple Guiting Manor in the Cotswolds was determined almost exclusively by the discoveries made by historic research, intuition and serendipity. The house was noted in the Domesday Book in the 11th century, making it one of England's most valuable buildings. I felt very conscious of the responsibility to the past and for making the gardens appropriate to the place.

I know the Cotswolds area very well. From the Middle Ages onwards it was a very wealthy region, with its wealth based on the production of sheep wool. The villages were connected by myriad sheep droving tracks, and discovering these lost track ways on old maps of Temple Guiting and the ghosts of old farm buildings now vanished allowed me to re-create the medieval structure of the ancient farmstead, with all its old walls and enclosures for animals. These eighteen 'rooms' now host the different gardens, and the proportion and flow feel right for the place. The actual garden designs that I created within the rooms owe nothing to the past, yet they feel comfortable set around this historic skeleton.

A great deal of statutory permission is needed for buildings as important as Temple Guiting. In part it was the proof found in old maps that allowed the extensive redevelopment to go ahead. After many years of work we were lucky to win a Drystone Walling Association Pinnacle Achievement Award for the extensive new garden walls. None other than HRH The Prince of Wales, the patron of the Dry Stone Walling Association of Great Britain, presented the Award amid bunting and tea in the marquee. Maps led us there.

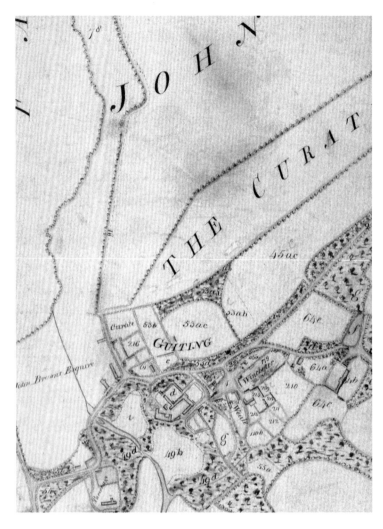

The maps indicate clearly the cluster of houses and farms and their trackways, fields, rivers and orchards. This is how I solved the riddle of Temple Guiting.

The largest part of the house in the foreground is two dovecotes (OPPOSITE). Stomachs were more important than bedrooms! The garden is built in what was a vast kitchen garden that would have fed the household in the 1400s.

This is an ancient sheep-droving track that passed between the various walled enclosures and led out into the 'wolds' (OVERLEAF LEFT). I love the structure the old tracks give to the garden, passing by the barn and the granary through orchards to the fields. We didn't restore the cow byre (OVERLEAF RIGHT) – I love its simplicity and fringed the old cobbled floor with achillea, thyme and *Stipa tenuissima*. The worn oak timbers and old mossy roof are enough.

The anti-garden
husbandry versus wildness

———————

What is wild? Gardening is on the luxurious fringe where the earth has been tamed and there is sufficient spare time to start embellishing it. It fascinates me that there is presently a fashion for 'wild' gardening. Wilderness has captured the gardening imagination. To garden is to create, to imagine and to tinker, so professing it 'wilderness' seems a bit counterintuitive. However much we wish to create the wild, it can only be a construct and is therefore, in my opinion, always a garden.

It is quite clear from the site plan that making a 'wild' garden still requires a lot of structure. Or at least in my mind it does. One of our starting points was that we didn't want to replace the hard landscaping from the previous garden, so I chose to subvert it. The old garden had set up some proportions that I then respected and it fell easily into making several large square 'rooms' of differing character. I built the tennis court with brick 'oast house' turrets on the corners to break the huge linear walls and to echo the oast houses of the area. Structure on plan becomes invisible in reality but is vital nonetheless.

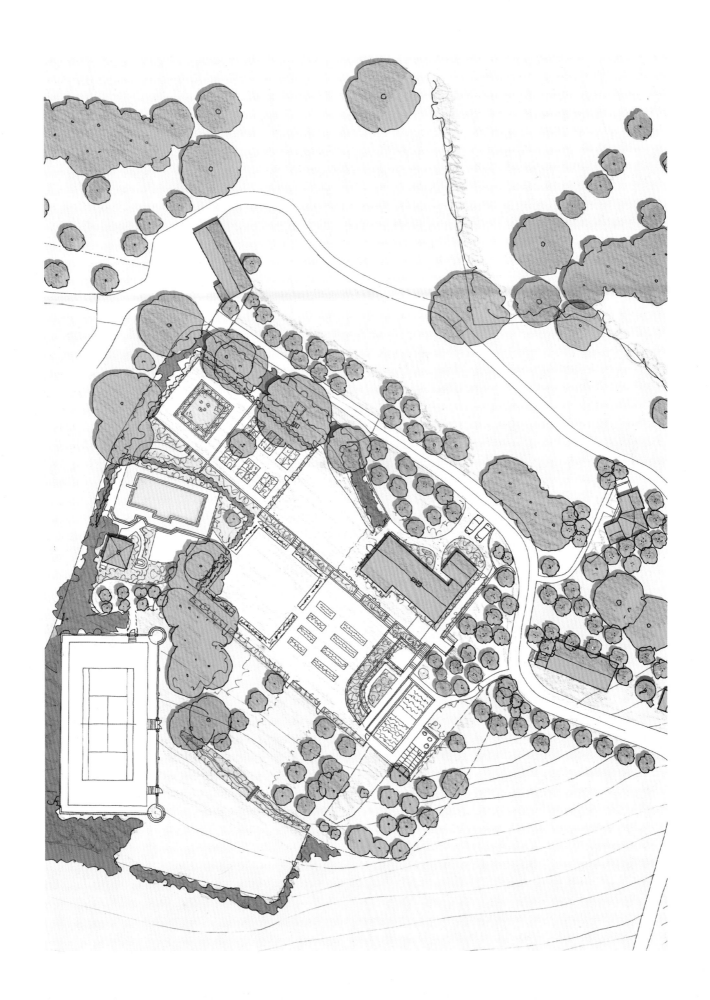

I have made a wild garden so I feel able to discuss this point from a position of experience. The owner, a free-thinking academic, wanted to subvert a perfectly logical garden that surrounded her Tudor farmhouse in the country into something altogether wilder. She wanted her children to enjoy the experience of boundless nature rather than acres of manicured lawn.

This act of subversion required thought. How far were we prepared to go in 'letting go' the land? I cautioned that it would be very hard to wrest it back from nature – visions of Thomas Hardy's furze cutters, coarsened by the relentless hacking back at the unremitting tide of gorse in *The Return of the Native*, have never left me!

The area was a recently decommissioned dairy farm. All the farm buildings had been removed and grassed over by the time I arrived. What lurked beneath the grass was anyone's guess. The land surrounding ours was beautiful, heavy iron-rich clay cloaked in sweet chestnut coppice, studded with sheets of bluebells in spring and wild stands of *Dryopteris filix-mas* and *Asplenium scolopendrium*. Coppicing creates a wild garden that is hard to better.

Both of us had independently known the splendidly learned entomologist and champion of research into schizophrenia Dame Miriam Rothschild and her remarkable house, Ashton Wold in Northamptonshire. Miriam had allowed her house to become subsumed by climbers until it became a vast green hairy mound with, at night, yellow flickering light emitting from the occasional window deeply recessed within the mountainous climbers. Her lawns had gone to long grass dotted with wildflowers and orchids, and there were birds everywhere. We came up with the idea of an 'anti-garden'.

Inspired, we would let the lawns grow unchecked, plant an 'Orwellian' vegetable patch, on the front lawn outside the drawing room in order that radishes were easily accessible, submerge the house in roses and vines and creepers and turn the rest over to masses of orchards and nutteries. The gardener went pale.

The layout required a strong underlying design to hold the whole rationale together. I planted wild nutteries, managed nutteries, orchards, coppices and a herbaceous border (a border of herbs!). And I smothered the house, the cottage and the oast house completely in *Rosa* 'Madame Alfred Carrière', *R.* 'Rambling Rector', *R. banksiae* 'Lutea', Virginia creeper, *Vitis* 'Fragola', *V. vinifera* 'Purpurea', with oxeye daisy everywhere. It was so exciting. There was such an abundance – of bees, butterflies, birds, slow worms, you name it.

The anti-garden has stabilized nicely into a simple system of management. Perhaps the greatest successes were the reverted lawns and the submerged house, and the vast quantity of relaxed wildlife they support.

Happily, the house and terrace are gradually being subsumed by planting (PAGES 38–39). I chose self-seeders, such as the *Erigeron karvinskianus,* thymes and catmint with 'blow-ins' of oxeye daisy to populate the terrace, while the climbers cascade down from the walls. *Rosa* 'Madame Alfred Carrière' covers two sides of the clapboard house and has currants and raspberries at her feet (OPPOSITE).

The garden had no mature trees so I went to Belgium and found a redundant fruit and nut research station that was closing down and bought everything they had. Knackered sixty-year-old trees gave instant aging to our plan (PAGE 40). Years of hard pruning had rendered them gnarled and strangely shaped, with dying branches here and there, but still sufficiently full of vigour to add to the garden. I planted nutteries because hazel slowly strips the strength from the fertile soil, weakening the grass and allowing wild plants to develop a toehold. I've let this process happen in real time (PAGE 44).

Lorryloads of colossal unclipped *Buxus sempervirens* 'Rotundifolia' gave depth to the empty spaces. The lawns in full untrammelled splendour have become very rich in species, despite the deadly clay. Bounded by great baulks of lightly clipped box, they are given a structured context (PAGE 41). Achingly beautiful, the little *Rosa* 'Stanwell Perpetual' toughs it out in the long grass (PAGE 45). She chugs on all through the summer, emitting a delicious scent.

The only vestige of gardening, other than the vegetable plot, is a very simple cutting garden for the house that is planted with near relatives of native species (PAGES 46–47).

Structuring

No garden can comfortably survive without a *strong skeletal structure*. Having walked the site and breathed in its character it is time to set to work with pencil and paper and consider the bones. Drawing a plan by hand evokes every aspect of the developing garden in your mind's eye. The pace and rhythm of the garden spaces, the views, the practicalities all settle into their rightful place. In shaping a plan all the real and invented intentions emerge. This is how the beauty of a place is *uncovered and made real*.

The necessary corsets

One of my seminal books about how to design is the excellent *Gardens are for People*, written in 1955 by Thomas D. Church. It is a brief and beautifully written book by a man who pioneered domestic landscape architecture in post-war America. Just as Abraham Maslow had set up the Hierarchy of Needs so ably for psychologists, so Thomas Church set up the abiding structure of fundamental truths for budding landscape architects.

Firstly, he discussed the need for unity, integrating the flow of movement between house and garden. This is followed by functionality: never neglecting the practical uses of a space so all members of the household are treated to pleasing areas of both service and recreation. He believed the economic and aesthetic success of a design relied on simplicity. And, ultimately, scale was vital to the creation of an integrated design.

Church also bestowed another great confidence, and that was to make drawings conversational. I hand draw everything. I can only design in this way, as the process of thought to solution to pencil is the most fluent for me. Hand drawings are warm, inviting and collaborative, and appeal to a potentially nervous client. For a long period of time drawings are the only thing that exist about a scheme, so they become quite talismanic and need to hold the imagination until things can start on site.

'First we must destroy!' This is often my opening remark. In making a new landscape or garden all the obsolete things must first be swept away and the space considerably cleared. Every aspect of what is inherited at the dawn of a new garden has to be thoughtfully reviewed and evaluated. I am an old hand at it now, and sometimes forget how terrifying it is to the uninitiated to see me going through the place issuing death warrants. Badly misshapen, damaged or sick trees and shrub planting must go. On one estate I felled 90 per cent of the trees (with the relevant permissions, of course), and cleared the way to a spectacular view for the new house that was being built. Old fences and irrelevant sheds or structures must also go. I get in there like Genghis Khan and sweep all before me. One client looked aghast at the smouldering piles of grubbed out trees and shrubs, roughly ten separate bonfires grumbling away on a foggy autumn morning across his newly acquired parkland. I had, he said, reduced his home to Mordor. Then just a few months later he said he now completely understood why it had to be done. As the junk is removed it is possible to really see the value in what is left, and this is where the real work can start.

This town garden is surprisingly wild for its small size and needed strict controlling lines for it to be legible and livable (ABOVE). A strict management programme for the black bamboo keeps them looking smart. If you haven't got the patience to care for it – don't plant it.

This old cart lodge is hundreds of years old (PREVIOUS PAGES). The blank flint wall and rich rusty clay roof tiles make the perfect backdrop for a garden. I made huge hedges of *Rosa* Iceberg ('Korbin') around the three different garden rooms – they, and the building, formed the structure for the intimacy of the gardens. *R.* 'Honorine de Brabant' and lavender are all the decoration that these beautiful flint walls need (OPPOSITE). I structured the colours very carefully so the purpled leaf tints of the *Catalpa* x *erubescens* 'Purpurea' match the rose and lavender and link both gardens over the wall.

I enjoy order and the process of ordering things and initial aspects of the work are an absolute delight to me. Managing the question of where everything that has been asked for goes is extremely satisfying. The wish lists are formidable, and often include swimming pools, tennis courts, formal gardens and informal gardens, drives, lakes and ponds, formal water features, running tracks, garaging, woodsheds, woodchip boilers, chicken runs, stables, cutting gardens, jungle gyms, potagers, zip wires, yoga platforms, meditation walks … you name it! Even the lists for small town gardens can run into pages. I build buildings if they are needed, which they frequently are, and have also been called upon to cross the threshold into the interior and design kitchens, fireplaces, bathrooms and bedrooms; literally everything and the kitchen sink! I love this process and it translates down even to smaller gardens, such as my own in London. Where space is at a premium it is really important to make clear unsentimental judgments about what goes where and why. Every view matters, and in a small garden there is no margin for error.

Irrespective of size, I always make sure there is a base survey of the land with all the levels on it. I can't work without levels. The process of locating things on a plan is fluid at this stage, as it is just pen and ink. All the elements required in the garden can be easily moved about. Sometimes I'll cut out bits of card or even drive cars around to indicate structures and

The dark waters of a swimming pool are perfect for mirroring the house and anchoring the eye in the garden (ABOVE). We chose a graphite tile and the resulting waters are cool and calm.

A literal 'back of an envelope' sketch for my London garden (OPPOSITE). I wanted the luxury of walls and east/west terraces for morning and evening sun – and a moat. The structure is very evident, as the planting has just gone in. The desired focus onto the woodland beyond is achieved by stepping the walls down and framing the view. The planting will be very jungly once it gets going, as this is a hot shadeless south-facing plot on a hilltop.

This end of a walled garden is highly structured. (OVERLEAF). At low level a rampart of box tightly clipped into eggy shapes forms a screen. The box-headed limes are tough customers and swipe all the water – the area below them is hard to keep pretty and is better screened.

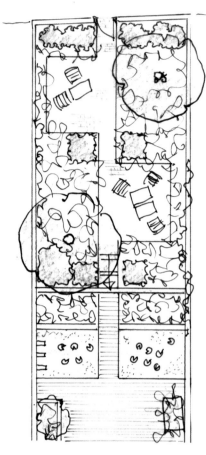

shuffle them around just to see how they feel in different locations. It is really important to allow quiet time for this process to take place. I almost always design in my private studio and rarely in the office. A technology-free environment is best for creative work. It is instinctive to see what is required to decongest a space and make it breathe freely. But this intuitive work has to be tested. Intuition followed by reasoned judgment is my process.

The proportion of space each activity or incident needs is different outside from the process when planning interiors. Experience tells me that we move differently outside – our gestures are longer, our gait changes, the way we sit in a chair outside in summer to have lunch has no kinship to the same activity indoors. We are relaxed, bigger, more generous and more expansive. Therefore, really consider how your space is meant to feel and scale it to the generosity of a big family group or the intimacy of a couple or single person reading in peace. Even in small gardens these changing dynamics are feasible.

Orientation
Understanding the elements

Three things cannot be hidden: the sun, the moon, the truth.

—BUDDHA

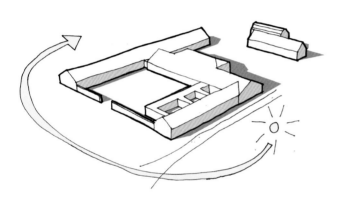

By drawing in the sun path for a plan, you graphically see the information you need to create a comfortable environment (ABOVE). I strongly recommend it.

I enjoy big bold shapes, and this topiary lawn was designed for parties (OPPOSITE). It looks amazing in all seasons, and the moving shadows trace the path of the sun. Each topiary piece is huge and that scale is vital to make it feel balanced with the buildings.

This house and its outbuildings blend seamlessly into the environment (OVERLEAF). All that is visible is the roof terrace and some chimneys. Soon they'll vanish too. The secret heart of it — the courtyard — is tucked away within sturdy walls. Protection from the equatorial sun is offered in the colonnade, and within the garden the yellow fever trees are raising their canopies and will provide light shade soon enough.

It seems pretty self-evident that understanding the sun and its impact during the day is important for a garden. Nevertheless, give it some time, as it is a more complex subject than it might first appear. For a start, it depends where on earth you are. We are living on a big spinning ball moving in orbit with other planets and we are orbiting the sun at some speed. That's a big enough thought to start with. The available sunlight and its intensity are therefore very different in relatively small geographic distances. I'm much less blasé about it all since living in the Mediterranean region and working abroad. It can catch you out. The sun path on the equator took a few minutes to understand!

Culturally people have different reactions to the sun. Mad dogs and Englishmen like to be out in the midday sun, but generally no one else does. Even in the UK it can be a mistake to orient a terrace or summerhouse to the south. It will heat up like a furnace in no time and be unbearable just at the time of year you wish to use it. East/west is best, with windows or shrubbery on both sides to let the light percolate through.

Terraces needs careful siting in order that they stay clement and warm without either baking or being plunged into perpetual slimy shade. I like formal terraces to have static large dining tables on them. To eat in full sun is very unpleasant, so choose an area that is warmed in the morning and becomes more protected as the day wears on. Sunbathing can take place on a lawn. My suggestion is to have light migratory furniture that can be easily carried from place to place so the choices between sun and shade rest with the individual.

Often there is little choice about orientation as a house already exists and has to be dealt with. I once designed two long borders as a pair heading off a west-facing terrace, both over 30m (98 feet) long, and then realized as I began the planting plans that one faced south and, inevitably, its twin faced north. Clearly the south side would be filled with rampant and volatile growth, as it got all the light, and the other side would be stable, cool and modest. I achieved harmony with a degree of ingenuity and rational planting, but I don't recommend it.

I do like north-facing sites. I love the quiet, still, shady calm of them. Topiary looks wonderfully static and ominous with long sharp shadows. I like to work in my north-facing studio with unvarying light. North is a gift.

The fundamentals of planning a layout
What goes where and why

Gardens must fulfil their many criteria through being well designed and beautifully executed. I look at the place scrupulously. By the time I leave at the end of the project the owners must feel that they are getting something that reflects them, not me. And, in turn, I must feel that I'm leaving something beautifully considered and exceptionally well built. Often a project contains many elements of design. In some cases it has been appropriate to design a rationale for an entire village, as was the case for one project in Norfolk and another in France, where three villages and five farming communities were brought into the scheme. The principles are the same for a tiny back garden; in fact the imperatives are almost greater, as nothing is ever out of sight. I recently made one that was only 4m (43 feet) square; it has to work hard.

How space is structured plays a huge part in how we feel. Early childhood sensations of fear, alienation and oppression that I felt in the dark red sandstone fire-bombed wreck of 1960s Coventry were just as intense as the joyfulness of playing by the river in the parks of my hometown or roaming the gardens at Hidcote were liberating. I still feel my way into a space now and listen carefully to my gut. It is a little like water divining.

I love doing these little axonometric sketches during the design process. They describe proportions so well. This is, in reality, a vast garden but on plan it looked minuscule due to the size of the parkland. Sketching really helps nail the proportions.

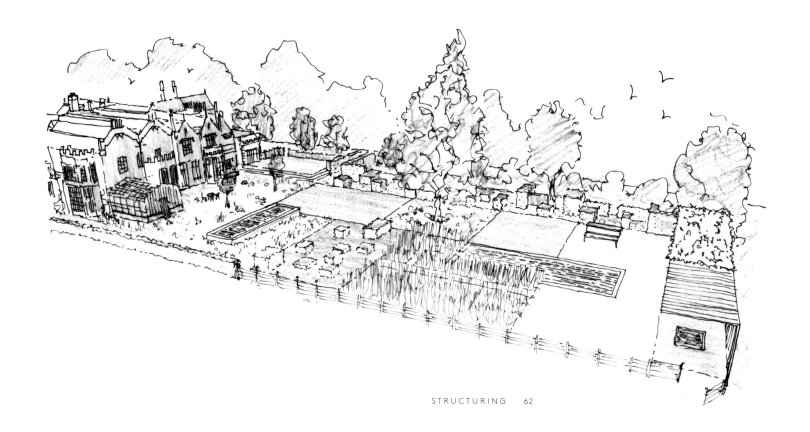

A view across a lily pond back to a big dining terrace captures the lovely changing light in this garden (LEFT). Water is so useful for bringing movement and life into large areas of planting. The opposite view from the terraces (BELOW) shows how the water creates foreground structure in this very flat landscape, breaking up the planting and echoing the cubed topiary – just a simple language of elements, none of which obscures the long view to the lake.

How to start a design? It is good to look at the subject in overview first. Don't worry about flowers or decorative accessories, as that comes much later on. Initially, the things that matter are the building blocks of the brief, and also all the items the client won't have thought of. I never let clients design a scheme. I incorporate all their ideas, of course, but then my role is to synthesize them and create a cohesive picture. My clients are intelligent and articulate people and usually very good at something very different. Subjects like drainage rarely crop up in a brief. Nor need they if you have a steady hand on the tiller and can bring the very many mundane subjects into the scheme competently.

Make sure you look out of all the windows on every floor and get a very good understanding from literally the inside out. Phrases that commit one to a hard act, such as 'blocking the view', don't work for me. Imagine you have a soft pencil in your hand as you look at everything and begin to shade out what you'd rather not see, and sharpen up that which you would like to emphasize. This gentler process brings into scrutiny where a view might be weak and unfocused, or a neighbouring building lumpy and heavy. I tend to view all other buildings as part of the landscape. The aim is to reach a balance of building to planting that is equally weighted and visually sensitive, much like the little villages on the rocks in France — a fusion of structure and softness. So in the initial layout we view from without and from within and place structures, walls, buildings, terraces, pools and so on in a coherent pattern that is agreeable from every vantage point. There should be a logical progression through a site and, if well executed, everything falls easily to hand, be it easy access for refuse collection or a grand reveal for the house. Don't be afraid to change ground levels or make sweeping architectural changes. If you can solidly justify it, then go for it.

I like to build up the drama and intensity in a design and often think it best to keep the approach to the house quite classical and simple. Position the outbuildings appropriately. Choose really good estate colours for doors and window frames, gates and railings and create a unique identity for the place. Make everything clear and legible. Build up some garden-y excitement around the front door that makes the visitor really want to get in. Gardens are all about the changing tempo of mood and activity, and these need to flow seamlessly, one into another. Once you are through the house, the show can really start.

Sir Edwin Lutyens was a wise man. He would listen politely to opinions on his designs and then carry on with his plans.

The extent of building on this Kenyan estate can easily be seen as we fly over — even so soon after finishing, the land is healing up again (ABOVE). This is no accident. It took 450 local people a year of work to cultivate, contour and grass up the land to our designs. The sensitivity of our builder, Ben Jackson, meant that the entire native bush was saved, and then we cultivated and planted rough grass and baby shrubs throughout (OPPOSITE). It's growing in speedily, despite the lack of water.

Protection
The inner sanctum

It is vital to feel secure in a garden. There is a special kind of serenity that can be found, knowing that you are alone, safe and engrossed in whatever activity moves you.

Gardens are unique in providing this. This feeling can be achieved in the design process. I like to structure a garden so that it ends up as a genuinely private refuge, a garden that is properly fortified by surrounding walls or hedges or buildings.

I have always very much liked monastery gardens and have visited lots over the years. They are sublime machines of functional good sense. Generally they are well sited next to a flowing river or brook that allows ample fresh water for pasturing cows, keeping trout and growing orchards with beehives. These activities lie outside the monastery walls – they are more public. Passing through the building you invariably find the inner sanctum – the cloisters, or 'claustrum' in Latin, meaning an enclosure. Here the monks could take their contemplative walks, probably after many long hours of gardening. In a garden the same meditative and tranquil condition can be found. There is nothing more engrossing than weeding, and it would be very unnerving to have the near-transcendental levels of concentration broken by an unexpected visitor.

In smaller town gardens, the effect is pretty much already in existence due to the natural enclosure of surrounding buildings, so it is just a matter of blending out unwanted views to amplify the serenity. In the city, I find that traffic noise or passing trains become secondary to the sound of birdsong when I am in that state of peaceful security.

A view through the courtyard gardens and the drawing room to the terrace – or, as I prefer to call it, the elephant ha-ha (OPPOSITE). The object of the whole project was to feel secure in the midst of raw nature and enjoy the proximity to it to the full. And, of course, make a significant contribution to conserving the wild animals we have left. Having made a protected garden it was no surprise when birds came and made their nests in the panicum (ABOVE). I feel foolishly successful when this sort of thing happens!

The drama of this view for me is the vast yew hedge I planted to make a protective boundary between the wild wood and the topiary lawns (OVERLEAF). I deliberately made it bulky and irregular so that it looked like it had been there since the 1700s. Apart from the self-sown ash trees on the right, every stitch of green was part of the garden project, even some of the roofs.

It is enormously seductive to be invited into a private place where few are ever admitted. I love making spaces that have the heady excitement of the harem about them.

You'd never think this was the centre of London and only seconds away from a globally significant sports centre (ABOVE). Yet it is a haven of peace and birdsong, and not another building is visible. It was quite an achievement within such a confined space.

This garden design made the best use of the old barn building and its huge doors to make the transition from an inner courtyard garden to the constructed meadows presided over by two ancient walnuts (OPPOSITE).

Our definition of a sanctuary has changed. We no longer hammer our fists on the door of a church in pursuit of protection. These days it's calm, quiet solitude and an escape from the rigours of city life we seek. Gardens have become vital to our sense of self-protection.

This site is enormous, bounded by roads on
two sides, a river on a third and a green lane.
The business end of the garden is squashed into
the top right corner and is even then, in reality,
a very large series of gardens.

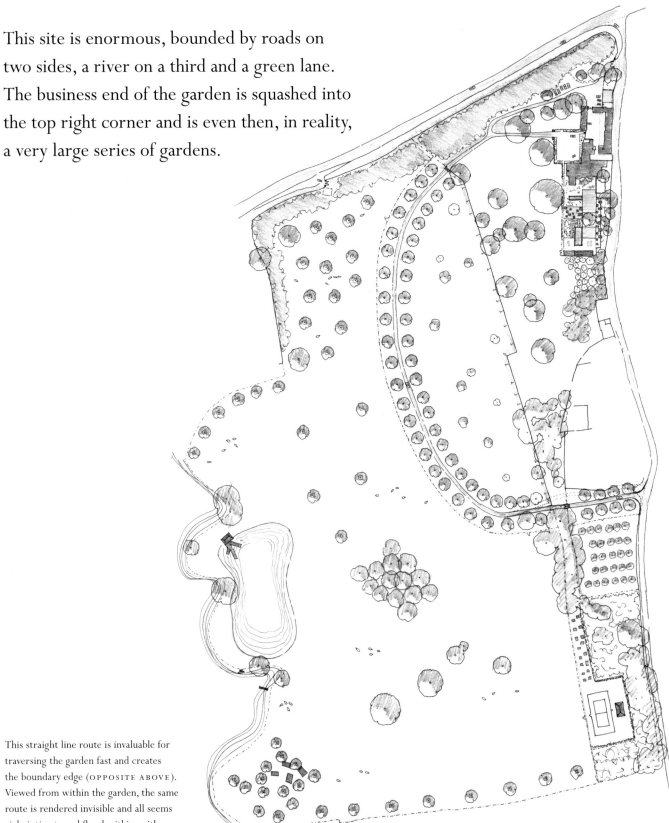

This straight line route is invaluable for
traversing the garden fast and creates
the boundary edge (OPPOSITE ABOVE).
Viewed from within the garden, the same
route is rendered invisible and all seems
rich, intimate and floral within, with
poetic reaches of English parkland
without (OPPOSITE BELOW).

Routes and views
Pleasurable repetition and far horizons

Once again it is not so much a matter of how much space you have as how it is defined. There are differing speeds of travel in a garden and it is worth making a little map of the animal tracks that will most obviously be used. It is pointless making a meandering path to a compost heap, as anyone staggering along with mountains of detritus just wants to get there fast! Sightlines from the house or special vantage points can be sketched in. Strong axial views generally radiate out from principal windows and address specific aspects of the landscape or special features. Smaller routes meander through shrubberies, woodland or herbaceous planting. I love very relaxed routes through herbaceous plants – it is seductive to feel immersed in planting with no boundaries. Mowing paths and patterns through grass is also a great way of creating soft routes and changing the tempo of a garden.

A rose pergola creates a linking route through the gardens to a walnut orchard (TOP LEFT). I designed the tiny gate and railing as a device to slow the eye.

This bucolic path was created out of a scruffy old boundary hedge left unkempt for years (TOP RIGHT). Strategic thinning, a gravelled surface and lovely woodland floor planting made it into something worth having.

This is the long walk to the tennis court (ABOVE). I used the drum rhythm of a Stevie Wonder track for the sizing and spacing of the cones, so that you can sing it and dance in time up the grassy path.

Sometimes a door is enough to create a dramatic change of tempo (RIGHT). I built the bastion beyond as the grand finale to the garden.

Somehow a propped open gate has always been a lure for me (PREVIOUS PAGES LEFT). This one rarely closes and forms part of the structure of the lovely house, hairy with Virginia creeper and yet strongly functional with its compacted gravel softened with planting.

It appeals to me no end to let paths shrink down to their most useful width. This one is actually much wider, but the cobbles have become colonized and we allow the climbing plants to flop over (PREVIOUS PAGES RIGHT). The seductive glimpse of steps leads one on.

I dreamed of this view from my first sighting of the property when awful trees obscured it and there was no bastion (BELOW RIGHT). Lady Getty and I were both born during total solar eclipses so I knew she would appreciate a 3.5m (12 feet) drop with no safety rail. She wrote the waiver and we enjoyed the purity of the result. We fed the wild red kites that she helped reintroduce here, as they swooped down on their great wings to take the carrion we held out.

I like to establish a hierarchy of routes and make the most of any exciting views at the same time. Posh routes come first — they are the ones that make visitors feel special as they are guided through the great moments of a garden. They lead one on through breathtaking moments and quiet idylls and are strictly separated from the functional routes. The practical routes allow mundane tasks to be carried out easily and without disturbing the tranquillity of others. I like to put them, if space permits, behind hedges or walls that lead to and from places where work takes place — greenhouses and vegetable plots, for example.

Finding where the good views are takes a bit of practice. Flat sites are very difficult to manage, as the eye has nothing to navigate with and so everything is seen at once. It is very important in these circumstances to make sure there are foreground, middle ground and distant views. Trees are the view-maker's friend, so do what artists do and make a frame with your hands and see what falls within your frame and set about planting out the rest.

As for how to avoid blemishes or blots on the landscape, such as your neighbour's horrible garage, just learn to look the other way, make a virtue and strength of alternative angles and before long you'll never notice it.

A feeling of security enhances the pleasure of a great horizon. I've always loved castles and the omnipotent feeling they give of viewing for miles in all directions. Harnessing this feeling is part of my garden-making lexicon.

Structures
Anchorage in a sea of green

Oast houses, once used for drying hops for brewing, are common in this part of England. By the time I'd finished wilding up the garden, this one rose turret-like above the surrounding woodland and made a useful structural contribution (OPPOSITE). This is a little detail of the roof of the shed built by the oast house (BELOW). Smothered in lichen, it sets off the *Rosa* 'Rambling Rector' to perfection.

Greenery, however beautifully designed and harmonized, can run the danger of being visually indistinct. In photographing gardens, it becomes obvious very quickly that without some kind of architecture or structure in the frame it is extremely difficult to give any sense of focus to planting. Returning again to the vision of the French hilltop village seamlessly welded into the landscape, it is easy to see why gardens need structures. Architectural elements are important to give depth to a scheme. To inherit a good cluster of roofs in an interesting composition is the ideal. If they aren't there, then they need inventing. Sometimes it can be as simple as reusing found objects. During one restoration we unearthed bits of steeple that had fallen from the church next door. I used one in a planting scheme and it instantly transformed a huge herbaceous border into something with an intriguing focal point. I also found a bit of old mullion window and a bell, and we remade these to sit on top of a newly built wall. This had the double virtue of aging down the newness of the garden and adding a little quirk to the views. At Manor Farm the problem faced was the lack of a distinct boundary between the house and the hill on which it stood. I stared at it for ages and then felt the only thing was to create a magnificent bastion wall with an 'infinity lawn' (see page 80). This anchored the house and garden and made the wonderful natural landscape even more focused and enchanting. Also, the spaces that existed between the existing buildings were too big. It wasn't feeling right either on plan or in person. I realized we had lost some farm buildings over time and that I needed another small roof back to balance the proportions of the garden rooms. I invented a little outdoor room and called it the Piggery. It feels right in the space and no one ever questions that it wasn't once a pigsty!

Tremendous natural boulder outcrops anchored one good city garden I made in New York. A fine 1920s house, perched on top of the boulders, and handsome mature oaks planted on the roadsides, framed the entire ensemble. The charm of the area is the lack of boundaries between the houses – instead of fences the houses all just seem to grow from the rocky hillside, and the woodland seems to naturalize the architecture, which, in turn, focuses the gardens (see page 81).

Originally, the holly tree seen at the right was in the garden but I sacrificed a chunk of garden and returned it to the field (ABOVE). I wanted to see sheep sleeping at the foot of the bastion and sheltering under the tree. That was part of the purpose of making such a strong statement with the bastion: sharp division.

I enjoy sharp lines. The structural benefit of these limes can be read from all over the gardens, and here in the walled garden they are quite pure and simple against the flint (RIGHT).

This New York house is built on a promontory of rock (BELOW). Sketching it out like this made me understand how amorphous this garden needed to be and that requires a skilled and sensitive landscaper who 'gets' it. The garden is nested into existing woodland over rock outcrops with no boundaries. The plants do all the work. I had a great time shoehorning them into crevices and making little secret dells in which one can dine al fresco.

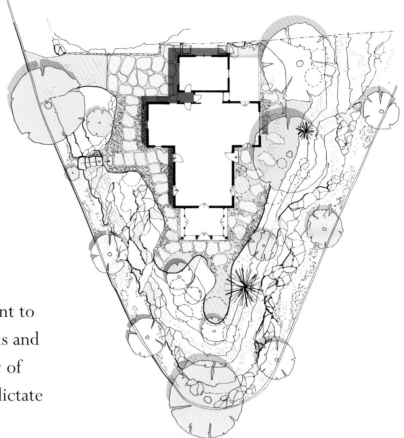

How generous and how confident to have built a suburb without walls and divisions and simply let the flow of underlying rock and the forest dictate the organization of the space.

Walls and boundaries
Containment and division

Gardens are just so much better when cleverly divided. The hide and seek of not knowing what happens next makes the experience playful and intriguing. Partitions can be used very effectively as methods of seduction. I have a door to nowhere in my London garden. I put it in the centre of the newly built wall at the end of the modest plot. The garden has the most tremendous views out onto natural woodland that is unprecedented luxury in the centre of a huge city. It amused me that I could make use of the classical visual play of extending my views and sense of ownership with a simple wooden gate. Almost without fail I'm asked what lies beyond the door. Boundaries also camouflage, and this same wall that helps so much with the sense of space and drama also helps disguise a weedy section of railway track. The wall is made of London brick and isn't particularly tall — just the right height to see over the top. If you can see over a wall, it isn't oppressive.

Choosing the height of a boundary is a language, and first it is necessary to know what you want to say. In the city I often like to be saying, 'My garden is much bigger than you think!' Layering the boundary can

The little 'Piggery' I built prevented the mid-air collision of the two sets of box-headed limes (BELOW). It would have been claustrophobic, I think, and this way there's the cheeky glimpse of the far horizon with its forest of pines.

Here is the infamous door to nowhere in my garden in London (OPPOSITE). I gladly sacrificed 60cm (2 feet) of land for the space behind it. Boundaries should go where you need them.

I made this fence of hazel wands and clay using a traditional pattern from Lesotho (OVERLEAF LEFT). I liked the juxtaposition with the razor-sharp, water-cut stone of the flower bed border.

In a profusion of rampant wild planting the only boundary is a rickety gate made from sweet chestnut (OVERLEAF RIGHT). It was inspired by rough animal fencing seen in Spain and by the locally indigenous chestnut palisade fencing.

The rear wall of the pool house was treated as an interpretation of the main façade, and creates a fractal arrangement of elements within it (ABOVE). It is a playful boundary and screens part of the boundary to the village that is now planted with orchard trees

The huge tree fern, *Dicksonia antarctica*, performs the vital role of allowing the necessary sharp corner of the garden boundary to be softened and diffused (LEFT). The terrace needs to be strongly defined, and the planting prevents the overall effect being harsh.

The softly muted flowers before it mellow the hint of brick and flint wall (OPPOSITE ABOVE).

Seen in the foreground is the oldest surviving wall in this very ancient garden – the house is mentioned in the Domesday Book (OPPOSITE BELOW). It gave rise to a garden of walls and partitions, many restored, and an equal number newly built in soft Cotswold stone.

have the effect of increasing the mystery and exaggerating the space. A Parisian friend worked with Alexandre Chemetoff on her small but historically significant garden. The house was built by Le Corbusier's teacher. Chemetoff made the garden remarkable by building perforated, pale brick screen walls within the boundary and then planting behind them. The effect is magical – no longer does the space feel small but rich and mysterious. Playing with scale like this is essential in gardens if they are to have any visceral impact.

Large gardens certainly need divisions in order to give them intimacy. These walls or high hedges don't necessarily need to fashion an entire room. Sometimes they simply form a single linear screen – something that creates a full stop, allows for decoration with climbing plants, and frames the trees behind it, perhaps. I will use hedging, masonry walls in many different styles or trained trees as partitions. Never be scared of scale. Big things work in both big and small spaces, so be adventurous and have some fun.

Green structure
Nature in the frame

A great deal of the structure of a garden is architectural: walls, retaining walls, paths and paving. I use trees, hedges and topiary as the second layer of building. They are my green architecture. My gardens look very structural on plan yet in reality they seem surprisingly soft and gentle. Gardens must stay beyond the whims of fashion. I have absolutely no problem with using elements that have been around in gardens since the dawn of time. We humans have the care of plants deeply ingrained in us, whether we like it or not. Not that long ago, it would have been an imperative in our chances of survival. I find that, without wishing to make blanket statements, if you hand anyone on earth a pair of secateurs, it will awake the latent pruning instinct! So my approach to green architecture is that it must be intelligently placed, it must have its roots in good ground and then it needs a person with clean sharp tools to care for it.

Placing and planting trees requires thought. It also requires a bit of reverence. Trees live from sixty years upwards, and often significantly into hundreds of years. In some ways, private gardens and parks in our increasingly urbanized lives might be their best chance of an undisturbed life. In any event, it is important to give due consideration to the species, soil, ultimate size and purpose. If planting parkland, choose an avenue species that is appropriate in scale. I use a lot of walnut, *Juglans regia*, for avenues, as they don't get too enormous and are very beautiful and productive trees. The native English lime, *Tilia cordata*, is another favourite. Consider the romance they will give in the future and choose accordingly. *Tilia cordata* is a very mercurial tree and every one, unless you choose a clone, is prone to grow into an unpredictable shape. I love that about it. Imagine in eighty years, when we are all long dead, the wonderfully crooked romance of a drive with pale green light filtering through the summer leaves.

Hedges are another favourite. I plant mile upon mile of hedges. For formal structure I'll use English yew, beech or hornbeam. They are the noblemen of hedging and suit most soils and circumstances. If the ground is complicated by poor soil, or is very wet then, of course, one looks elsewhere. The plant must suit the physical circumstances. That is a golden rule. I love hedges for their seasonal value, their sound-buffering qualities and their positive effect for birds. Poor birds. They have so few undisturbed places left to live and a good solid hedge is like a premium condominium.

The number of notes that exist for us to write our tunes with are pretty much set – the rest is in the hand of the composer

A loose sketch is usefully descriptive. I had to cover a significant distance with a route and thought a graphic hedging treatment would be interesting. The strict lines of high hornbeam hedge are not just graphic but also work as a windbreak on this devilishly windy site. It is 3m (10 feet) tall and continues to wrap around the tennis court. The topiary sits in long grass that has recently been cut.

Where would we gardeners be without topiary? I grew up near a remarkable Elizabethan garden, Compton Wynyates, in Warwickshire, now sadly stripped of its topiary. We would sometimes walk there through the woods. The excitement of coming up through the undergrowth to the crown of the hill was met with the most amazing display of topiary on the front lawns. I don't think I've recovered yet, as I still love to plant topiary lawns. I use topiary wherever it seems justified. It anchors views, creates spaces and adds humanity to a garden. It feels like people, old friends. I'm planning a new topiary garden for myself and it promises to be unusual.

Topiary in winter earns its keep, casting strange figures in the ominous chill of the landscape (ABOVE). This time of year reminds me of the winter paintings of Johan Christian Dahl, the great Norwegian landscape painter.

This garden is often described as very floral (OPPOSITE BELOW). The truth is somewhat more complex, as can be seen here, with many layers of structural planting holding in quite narrow beds of voluminous prettiness.

In order to appreciate the stunning views, this garden needed to be held tightly to the foreground (OVERLEAF). I planted a fluffy native hedge on the boundary to tie in to the woodland opposite, then punctuated the rose garden with cones of yew. All green, all soft. The romance is in the lavishly unpopulated countryside.

Taxus baccata, the English yew, is a tree of great antiquity and can live to at least 4,000 years. It deserves our respect.

This little garden is the last in a sequence of eighteen walled gardens within a whole (RIGHT). It is a small enclosure that would have been a pigpen or a cow byre. It needed something structural so I chose pig topiary. A rare moment of humour in the serious business of gardening.

Water
The magic ingredient

In the Loire Valley in France, my favourite chateau, Chenonceau, was built in 1547 as a place of aristocratic serenity. We went when I was about five or six. Nothing I'd ever seen in England came anywhere close to this staggeringly beautiful chateau and minutely managed landscape garden. Nowhere is a house and landscape more ingeniously created and fortified than here. The great flat gardens – the very antithesis of subtle English gardens – lay as ornamented plateaux before the glistening white chateau with its silky grey slate turrets.

Across a slender bridge the chateau sits astride the smoothly flowing river. I had never seen a building treated as a bridge, its beauty amplified by its own narcissistic reflection in the slow-moving water. Looking at the chateau these days, with everything drawn in CAD and modelled in 3D software, one is hard-pressed to conceive of something so sublimely precise being made by hand from pale blocks of limestone nearly 500 years ago. I wonder what the drawings looked like? Or even if there were any. I marvelled at the stanchions – how could such a huge building be able to stand in water? I spent a lot of time in rivers, and the bottom of ours at home was treacherously squelchy mud, many feet deep. Here it seemed that the feet of the building were secure in their aquatic depths. My first foray into structural engineering ensued, as I couldn't sleep until I'd found an answer. How was the water held back from the river to enable building?

As philosopher Lao Tzu is reputed to have said, nothing is softer or more flexible than water, and nothing can resist it.

How could people work in these conditions? I knew that one isn't supposed to build a house on shifting sands either literally or metaphorically. Stability for the building was as important as the roots of an oak tree, and that tangible stability transmitted itself as a feeling of confidence to me standing on it and staring down into the river. Structure. Everything is made confident by structure. This beautiful castle taught me a great lesson.

Water is the very stuff of life. In the old days we would have made provision for finding, collecting and storing it close to our homes. Lancelot 'Capability' Brown, the great English landscape architect, undertook water management on large estates and elevated this singular skill in water engineering to the level of an art form. Almost as a by-product of the prodigious land-moving required in creating lakes and canals, he sculpted fashionable landscapes for the great and the good. I love the anecdote that he even found time, when called upon, to fix the drains in Green Park, London.

These are the lead spouts I created for myself at home in my moat (ABOVE). The house has a history of old lead pipes springing leaks and I like the idea of commemorating them.

There is something magical about crossing water, and in Africa where water is so scarce it is a luxury. The stepping-stones lead to a terrace cooled by the pool (OPPOSITE).

As any landscaper worth their salt knows, a prodigious quantity of water is needed to make a good landscape. If the opportunity presents itself, I like to start with a river or a stream. Nothing betters natural water flowing through a garden, and by gently opening up the banks and moderating the light levels, nature will create all the beauty for you. Next to this comes the building of lakes or large ponds. A house in the country must have water. Water anchors the eye. Water brings light and reflections. Water hosts life. I was once told that a newly made lake left completely unplanted would be fully colonized with plants, animals, birds, amphibians and bugs within a year. That is magnetism in action.

In Kenya we managed water from the outset of the project. We repaired a vast dam so that the biennial rains could fill it. A borehole was dug but gave very minerally water – too strong for plants, as the minerals burn their leaves. I put some small water troughs with water lilies in them through the central courtyard garden and also a more formal canal of water. Water is so precious here that it becomes extraordinarily magnetic. No sooner had the bowser filled the troughs with fresh water from the dam than we were dive-bombed by swirling house martins. They began nest-building in the courtyard colonnade the same afternoon. Swiftly on their tail feathers

Swimming pools are so versatile and this one is in a very natural garden, so I planted hedges of raspberries for snacking on and let the grass grow long and wispy (ABOVE).

This old farrier's pond was perfectly circular on old maps, so I re-created it the same way (OPPOSITE ABOVE). This is amplified in winter and accentuated by the knobbly fists of the willow pollards. In summer the pond is brimming with life (OVERLEAF). It has ducks, newts and frogs as regulars. Dragonflies of huge size breed there and I've seen slow worms swim across. In summer it is a mirror for the sky, and in winter it is graphically returned to its original form.

Before we could do anything in Kenya we needed to make sure there would be water, so we fixed the dam (OPPOSITE BELOW). A very long wait ensued, as rainy seasons produced nothing. Then, suddenly, it was full. I find this little image very moving. Water is so precious.

came the gigantic neon dragonflies, then bees, then butterflies. How do they know to come? When we dug and filled the waterhole down in the lugga, the guys had to run like crazy to higher ground, as out of nowhere came the heavy thunder of buffalo feet. Buffalo are the scariest of the wild animals that roam the high country of the Rift, and there is no stopping them in pursuit of their aims! The water is mesmeric and they all come immediately. It must carry a very strong scent that we blunt-nosed humans can hardly discern.

I can't make a garden without water. It brings the seasons in, and is often a magnet for wildlife.

An ordered estate
the well-tempered parkland

OXFORDSHIRE

———

Sometimes a place reaches a point where everything needs looking at and a comprehensive restructuring can be considered. This was one of these. The entire estate needed rationalizing. My favourite assignments are where I can consider every element of how a place works and then put it all into practice. Making the garden knowing that I've made sure everything around it is functioning beautifully is a dream come true.

The area shown in the sketch plan is the heart of a much bigger estate (see plan page 72) and this is where I concentrated the gardens. Siting a pool and pool house opposite the principal façade allowed me to make a very structured space. I could devise a magnificent entrance courtyard, and by building a traditional stone-roofed building as a garage I also created a lower courtyard at the rear. This means everything pleasantly domestic is close at hand, secure and focused. Once a space is rationalized, the beauty of it begins to appear.

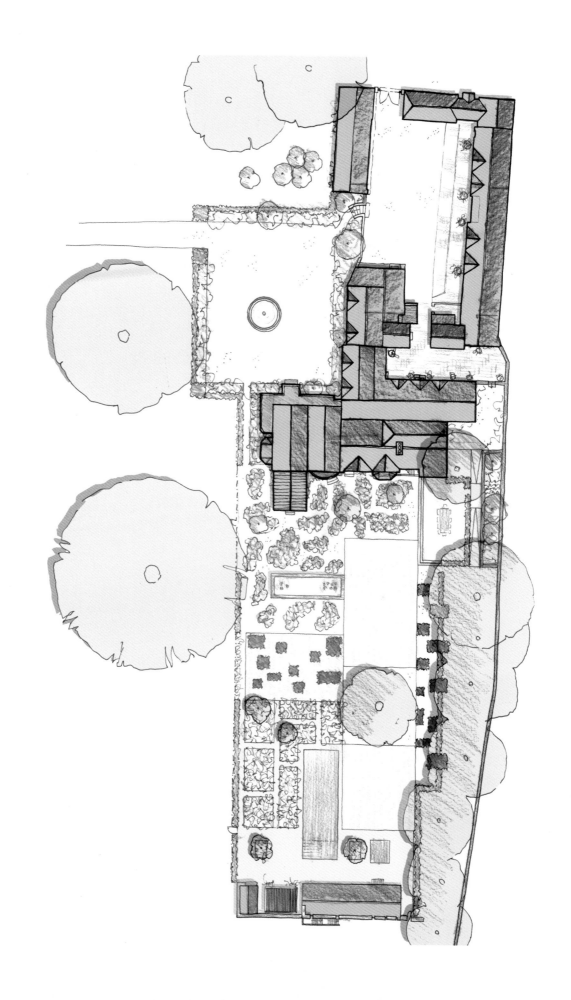

The estate is huge. It is also flat. Flat land is challenging to design, as everything is visible in one go. It becomes hard to hide things that need hiding, and creating focal points is necessary to hold the eye. This estate was full of potential, with some ancient parkland trees and a brown trout river. It was enjoyable bringing these elements back into prominence and working out where to put everything else to make it work smoothly.

I have a golden rule that wherever possible we don't take spoil off site but reuse it. In this instance the restructuring of the estate involved reusing mountains of spoil, especially from the digging of the swimming pool. This allowed me to introduce gentle contours over the landscape and also to hide the newly designed gardener's compound and boiler houses behind pretty hillocks covered with trees. This protected the views from the house. The new drive passes seamlessly through parkland devoid of eyesores, and the house and new pool garden have wonderful vistas in all directions.

The most important thing in structuring an estate is remembering that the gardens that are used every day must be close to the house. I always like to put the fun things near at hand, so using them becomes intuitive and easy. This is a social house and there are lots of friends and family around, so plenty of cooking goes on outside, and the pool gets used all year round. I chose to use it as an ornamental part of the garden. I suggested that we place the pool house facing back to the main house and utilize the pool as a reflecting pool. The architects and I are old friends and our collaborations are really enjoyable. We reached easy agreements about most things, which always ends up in a better outcome.

Swimming pools can become very attractive in a garden, and in this one I wanted the swimmer to experience the garden. Two sides of the pool are set within huge beds of perennials segmented by smooth stone paths. I had visions of the children running through these paths, playing hide-and-seek, wet from their swimming. On another side of the pool is a lawn for sunbathing and picnics, and at the shallow end is the terrace with the pool house and outdoor kitchen.

The main house is completely wrapped in sumptuous planting emerging through gravel. I created a huge terrace off the kitchen that sits slightly elevated above the main gardens, with commanding views out over the gardens and parkland towards the new lake. Enveloped in soft planting, this is a lovely place to spend Sunday afternoons and to appreciate the beauty of the landscape spread out on all sides.

Before I started there were no focal points and no structure in the estate. The gift of the place is the magnificent, if slightly battered, parkland trees – the cedar, limes, oaks and beech (PAGES 102–103). After some remedial work to stabilize the cedar it became the encircling arm and background character to the new garden.

Even in very loose planting there needs to be some backbone strength. Tucked into the summer madness surrounding the house are sun-loving evergreens such as cistus, box and cryptomeria (PAGE 104). The structure of colour compatibility is used so that the foreground herbaceous planting has plenty of green to anchor it into the wider estate, with its predominantly green hues (PAGE 105). The planting is muted with flashes of crimson and orange to spark it here and there. The structuring continues in the big beds (OVERLEAF). I admire huge perennial borders yet I'm a shrub-layering type, as I need the winter structure rising to the mid-height. The backdrop of topiary cubes gives weight and depth, and frequent stands of *Calamagrostis* x *acutiflora* 'Karl Foerster' support the more fleeting floral elements.

This area of the garden was generated by the existing clump of *Crinum* x *powellii* tucked into the corner of the Georgian conservatory. I'd never seen it so big and healthy! So the garden was then structured as a semi-exotic planting through gravel. It's relaxed, easy to weed and stays warm, so the plants love it (OPPOSITE ABOVE).

I like a swimming pool to feel part of a garden, so this one is embedded into huge plant beds at one end and has a pergola and outdoor kitchen at the other (OPPOSITE BELOW). The sandstone is warm and inviting underfoot.

Harmonizing

Gardens are all about the lives of others. They make perfect settings for all the excitements of life, large and small. By using a *carefully selected palette of ingredients* for a garden it is possible to make something that harmonizes perfectly with its position. Designing with the right choices of materials allows the garden to settle seamlessly into place. Seeing a design intimately welded into the landscape is a joy I always strive for. The old adage of never using more than three materials in a scheme struck a deep chord with me, and runs like a heartbeat through the work. Materials that are fluently understood and confidently used mean the end result will sing.

Loving the tune

The door to my garden in France is over a little culvert that flows down to power the walnut mills in the medieval town (BELOW). In autumn when the nuts ripen, the rivers rise and the watermills creak into action to make walnut oil. Effortless engineering and visual harmony.

This is the route to a turf-roofed sauna (OPPOSITE). I didn't want to build anything too overbearing so just adopted Neolithic detailing and rafted a walkway across the marshy ground. It's thrilling to be able to walk over impossible ground and see the life that goes on in it.

There's something of *Little House on the Prairie* about this that I could never have anticipated (PREVIOUS PAGES). I think it's due to the rather un-English pitch of the cedar shingle roof. The flowery mead has been a big success and the harmony created between weathered timber, wise old trees and drifts of colour is beautiful.

Always start by going for a walk locally. Understanding a location is really at the very heart of good design, and the sponging up of information that can occur on a quick amble is priceless. Often I find that the combinations of materials I notice as being particularly beautiful are the product of either an accident of building or immediate necessity. One of our urban projects has a stretch of wharf wall to the river. Originally built over a hundred years ago in brick, it was later fixed – obviously in a time of financial trouble – with roughly poured ballast concrete. The result is strangely beautiful. Coarse and misshapen, it has become colonized by Virginia creeper and little mosses. I look longingly at it knowing it would be impossible to replicate, as it was thrown together with urgency and thoughtless freedom.

The English village where I live is very old indeed and has been built and rebuilt over hundreds of years. Far from being just an historic relic, it is also a contemporary community and has some amazing examples of 1960s Brutalist architecture, and more recently prominent modern buildings have been grafted onto spaces between the older cottages and villas. This results in some striking and unexpected combinations of materials and expressions of style. It appeals greatly to my aesthetic freedom. Because of the interconnectedness of the village houses the gardens all seem to blend together and tie everything into a homogeneous whole. All materials can, therefore, be attractive if sympathetically combined.

Gardens are a great environment for personal expression and experimentation. In the space of a few metres in the village there is a very correct English garden with immaculate lawns, pleached lime trees and pretty gravelled paths. Next door is a hugely imaginative Italianate garden that the owners have made over forty years, with terracotta-tiled paths in intricate designs, mosaics, extravagant urns and classical sculptures. This freedom of personal expression is made possible with the imaginative use of materials.

It sets my teeth on edge if I see the wrong stone used in the wrong place, or a jumble of different types of stone paving all mashed up together. Understanding local materials is always a good way to start. Spending a little time discovering if you are in an area with a particular type of stone or brick is a good preparatory point to a comfortable design.

I'm working up a scheme that marries together very tall old mellow stone walls with some original old red brick walls. The two colours and textures blend beautifully together and so I've determined to continue with the same stone type – albeit newly quarried and newly cooked soft red brick. A friend, the historic buildings architect Ptolemy Dean, taught me that it's better to use new bricks made in a traditional way than source reclaimed. Ptolemy always advocates using new materials for historic schemes. The traditionally made bricks will age beautifully and very quickly, whereas the reclaimed will always retain that beaten-up look. Of course, if beaten up is what you are after, then that's a perfect fit, but in this instance, against an interesting historic house, it would look cheap.

At the same house I've been looking at ways of detailing a large courtyard. To have an unbroken expanse of gravel would look unfocused. I chose to add a perimeter pavement as a border to the gravel – about 1m (3 feet) wide of rough-hewn stone cobbles. This is quite a traditional response, as these cobbles would have originally been used as stable floors or routes to outbuildings. They are completely in keeping. We make them from rough new walling stone, lay them on edge and chisel them back so they are comfortable to walk on. They would look at bit too rustic in front of the grand entrance, so here I switch to using opulent great slabs of beautifully sawn stone from the same quarry. I have been told that I specify stone slabs 'at the limit of human endurance'! And I respond that if people didn't make the effort, we wouldn't still be enjoying the Pyramids in Egypt!

Small courtyards can take a lot of detail, as they are intimate spaces and prettiness is valuable. I discovered one of my favourite details in a very old house in the country. At first, I couldn't quite work out what I was looking at. Tiny pebbles set in moss? No, wrong colour and the texture wasn't stony. It turned out to be sheep knuckle bones. I did more research and found that in the 18th century bone was often used as a paving material. It must have been plentiful and cheap. If you aren't a vegetarian, it can be an interesting option, but probably quite tricky to source these days. So instead I've used small pebbles. Pebbles are plentiful and cheap, although a fiddle to lay nicely. Lots of decoration isn't my thing so I avoid swirling patterns and many colours. I just like one or two sizes in the same colour and then set out simple geometric patterns that relate to the space. Once they are settled with pots full of plants placed on them, they resolve into a timeless beauty.

It is important to consider the effect our consumption of materials has on our world. This tends to underpin my choices. I'd rather use local materials because they are visually harmonious and will tend to be appropriate in more ways than one. They suit the local climate, they don't travel far and as they age and degrade they simply fall back into the earth they rose from.

I invited David Wilson, the great Scottish stone artist, to make this chalk drystone wall for me (ABOVE). I'm obsessed with the qualities of chalk and it blends so beautifully with the planting – all chalk tolerant.

I'm a fan of straightforward methods of making things. We made this very squat heavy gate from two layers of oak planks clamped together with iron studs (OPPOSITE ABOVE). This is a traditional way of making doors and the advantage is that it's very hard to hack through it with your sword. No one wants to blunt their weapon! More oak planks and some chicken netting ford a flooded ditch (OPPOSITE BELOW). This couldn't be simpler really.

Water, walls, trees and the billowing planting of the cutting garden all combine into one misty whole (OVERLEAF). On plan this garden looks highly structured (see page 37), yet here it is easy to see all of the elements in harmony.

I've an Armenian friend who is an eminent master woodcarver. He began carving at the age of four at his grandfather's knee. Skills with tools and understanding the properties of different woods ran fluently through his veins before he even reached the age of apprenticeship.

Creating context
In search of clarity

It is really important to think about what you're trying to create. Whatever materials are chosen must have a strongly thought-through rationale and appropriateness to the place.

I love huge flagstones. On one project I had them cut at 1m square (10 square feet) in rich thick sandstone. The house is old but the paving needed to be brand spanking new and designed in a contemporary way, as it ties a modern stone-built pool house to a big graphite tile-lined swimming pool and also the house (see page 54). Using a rustic finish stone would make it ungovernable and the detailing of the stone was extremely precise. The garden sits between the old house and the new pool house and I chose to place the buildings facing each other, so the pool can act as a reflecting pool to the magnificent castellated façade of the old house. The landscaping is creating an entirely new context for all the elements. I chose to use a stone very similar in colour and texture to the original house, but expressed it in a very different way. The house is big and imposing, hence making the slabs very large and the terraces sizeable too. The stone needs to balance the house and look meaningful and generous. The detailing on the stone is minimal and precise. We spent a long time creating perfect corners for the pool. Many people won't notice these little details, yet they make all the difference to the serenity and quality of the end result. And I notice!

Working abroad is always interesting. In Kenya we had to invent a context for the building and that work falls squarely in the lap of the landscaping. With a newly built house I work alongside the architect and find materials that not only suit house-building but also the landscaping. These early complicit decisions mean that the end result will be coherent. There is a beautiful material called Meru stone. As always with an unknown material, it is vital to test it – look at it sawn and rough, wet and dry. This volcanic stone looked really good with a rough surface but awful when it was sawn. So that decided it. It could only be used rough and as it only came in small pieces we were restricted to that. However, this wasn't an impediment. Again I used a design that I took from my knowledge of France. Streets in our medieval village are made of pale limestone chunks, worn smooth over hundreds of years. I replicated this in Meru stone in Kenya and complemented it by cutting the steps out of the natural rock just below the surface. This blending of small stone with the rock anchored the scheme effortlessly.

The more you think about a suite of materials the more obvious the right choices become.

This cloister in Kenya is so pleasingly balanced and timeless you have no sense that it's only just been built (ABOVE). I enjoyed creating the paving with tiny rills either side to take the monumental rains away as fast as possible.

The inspiration for much of my work comes from observing the world. This is a rocky path in my hometown in France (OPPOSITE).

In the Cotswolds and minutes away from the *ne plus ultra* of Hidcote it is easy to feel self-conscious as a designer. I felt the gardens at Temple Guiting should be in the high ideal of English Romanticism and I emulated that Edwardian feeling here in the long borders of the Granary Walk (OVERLEAF).

I think Albert Camus got it right when he said harmony is a matter of how a man lives his life — harmony is happiness.

Pausing on the Granary Walk, it seemed a view was needed to break it up (OPPOSITE). The interrelationships in the garden need to be made frequently for the place to feel comfortable and inviting. I use doors for this — a sudden sweeping view to the far horizon is captivating. A local quarry was reopened to provide stone of the right hue. We dressed it into blocks for the walls and crushed it for the gravel. It is of the place and of itself correct.

Wooden gates can be as varied as their locations dictate, and around this farmhouse the local material is coppiced chestnut (ABOVE). The wood is humble and used for inexpensive temporary fencing, and that's how I decided to use it in the wild anti-garden. I designed a really simple gate with a slight detail of varied height at the top, and left the gates propped open in the long grass. They just settled into their bucolic setting and relaxed there.

Texture and colour
Sympathetic magic

Natural materials age gracefully, taking on interesting patinas that add beauty to a garden. This process can't be rushed. I am very careful about what I retain in a project. At Temple Guiting – an exceedingly old house – virtually everything had to be built from scratch or repaired. It worried me that the end result might look too new and too harsh against the old building, so I kept as much as I could of the ancient fabric of the gardens. In particular we had a very battered old gate hanging in a tired old frame. I kept it exactly as it was. The paint on the frame had weathered to a chalky soft pink – a colour almost impossible to replicate. It sits beside the creamy, flaky old Cotswold stone. I loved the soft colour combination and chose to tone the planting into it – soft pink roses and achilleas at their feet. It is a gentle moment in the garden and made stronger for the underlying thought.

Oak takes on a character as it weathers down that is absent when it is newly worked. I made an oak pergola with leaded post caps and wrought-iron hoops to carry some climbing roses. It looked good on day one, but fifteen years later the oak has mellowed as the tannins have washed away and the surface sealed. The lead caps have the traditional milky bloom on them now they are settled and have become more beautiful. I pay a lot of attention to the colours of materials in a garden. Wood and stone harmonize very easily, and it's worth getting to know them well before you use them to ensure that they do what you want as they age. I'm always looking at paving and stone used in urban environments and researching what it is. It will receive much more wear and tear than in a private place and so you get an accelerated insight into its behaviour over time.

Often the colours in a building material will influence my planting palette. New York bluestone in America lives up to its name. It is a strong deep slate blue with virtually no figuring in it. It influenced an entire planting of blues – I planted *Panicum virgatum* 'Heavy Metal' in great drifts beside walls of bluestone, shot through with occasional darts of orange *Aquilegia canadensis*. Much to my surprise the aquilegia attracted little hummingbirds that added darts of electric green. Nature often turns up as a fantastic randomizer, adding unexpected colour brilliance.

I designed these tiny gates and railings in tandem with Andrew Renwick, the master craftsman and owner of Ridgeway Forge (BELOW). Even a small detail well made lifts a garden to another level of sophistication. The deep strong Dutch blue sits perfectly with the stone buildings and Welsh slate on the roof.

Old Cotswold limestone and battered oak with ancient flaky paint needs little more than a weak pink achillea and puffy *Rosa* 'Blush Noisette' to complete the picture (OPPOSITE).

This house is so handsome it needed very little to dress it up (ABOVE). The front door is rarely used, so, inspired by my favourite painter Vilhelm Hammershøi, a few simple terracotta pots of pale species geraniums were enough.

Accessorizing I treat with caution, yet we had this lovely pot with an interesting patina on it. I stuck it in a bald patch where I'd removed some woody plants and enjoyed the focus it gave to the big bed (RIGHT).

A set of tiny yet beautiful railings and gates stops people pitching to their doom down the external cellar steps (OPPOSITE ABOVE LEFT). They add a layer of texture between planting and house and merit their inclusion.

This old piece of wall is like an artwork, even though it was originally thrown together by an impoverished farmer who used everything he could lay his hands on to build his cow shed (OPPOSITE ABOVE RIGHT). With the richness of the flint wall, I just needed texture and elegant planting, so chose a bench made of vine root and *Rosa* 'Mermaid', sweetly scented and constant flowering (OPPOSITE BELOW).

Oak, brick and flint have matured into beautiful textures and colours and formed the basis of my palette for the entire garden.

Making things
Getting your hands dirty

Some projects demand a new and unique approach. Spring restaurant at Somerset House in London was one of these. I sat discussing the new restaurant with Skye Gyngell, the talented owner-chef. Somerset House is one of London's great Neoclassical buildings and as such has a profound history. Skye was asking for a beautiful indoor dining atrium filled with olive trees, and as she spoke so poetically about her vision, my heart began to sink. Neoclassical it might be but conducive to outdoor olives it certainly wasn't! It was also quite tight for space if you take into account the hive of activity it would become. I could plant a conservatory garden easily enough but needed to make it special. I wanted to reflect the history of the building somehow. I chose to panel the walls with an artwork I devised. I collected fresh huge gunnera leaves from a friend's lakeside and reverse-cast them in liquefied marble dust. This material means they look like fossils, like giant crinoids. I felt we needed some sense of antiquity in the space that has the same sort of ambience as one of London's great museums. Framing the panels in bronze, I used bronze planters to balance the scheme. Cool marble and the richly patinated metal make a very chic combination. Gratifyingly, we won a rather grown-up award for it, beating off stiff competition from much larger commercial schemes around the world. It seems people respond well to the handmade quality of the space. It has an emotional sensitivity inherent in it that makes it comforting to be in.

On the subject of metal, I always like to design gates and railings for projects. In accordance with my tastes they are usually quite elegant and uncomplicated. Hand-forged metalwork is just so much more interesting than things made of components. All the forgery joins and rivets are so attractive. They are tactile, with their hammer marks and irregular tapers. And I commission mile upon mile of estate railing. This is the beautifully simple horizontal iron railing used on estates to keep sheep in place. The accessories run to field gates and tree guards, tree seats and all sorts, and I just love it. Quite often it really is keeping sheep out, and otherwise I use it in gardens as a transparent boundary that allows plants the freedom to grow as they please. There is something about the juxtaposition of roses and estate railing that makes a garden seductive and sexy. Gardens want sex appeal.

Sometimes I get quite high-tech with making things in stone. In London I wanted incredibly precise inlaid stone in a complex pattern for a terrace. This is very tricky CAD work that we spent a lot of time developing.

The tactile quality of the walls I made for Skye Gyngell's restaurant was the product of my desire to make things with originality and Skye's love of truthful ingredients (TOP). We won a prestigious landscaping award for the atrium. This was the leaf as we rolled it into the clay for casting (ABOVE). I like having my hands in the materials. You can never quite tell how an idea will perform so there is excitement in it.

I made this bespoke triad of stools for the Design Centre Chelsea Harbour with huge matching planters filled with trees (OPPOSITE). They are completely handmade and one-off. The seats are covered in Scottish Bute tweed. We won an award for the furniture and the installation, which was very gratifying

This is our very high-tech evocation of the landscape of Lesotho for Prince Harry's first foray into the Chelsea Flower Show (OPPOSITE). The sinuous contour line steps are based on the minutely terraced hills of Lesotho. I made the rock very mannered in our technical interpretation of that natural place (BELOW RIGHT). What is easy to conceive and sketch is a good deal harder to make real, and my colleagues Maude and Pernille took on the challenge. Maude's drawings for the terraced stairs are da Vincian in their complexity. The hard landscaping throughout shared one colour tone – pale dove grey. Lesotho is called the Sky Kingdom, so the interior of the rondavel terminates in a lens for viewing the sky (BELOW).

I made this extrapolated sculpture of three circles for the same garden (OVERLEAF). The first squared circle is a spare frame of bronze, the second a travertine-filled bronze frame with a void and the third a book-matched sandstone disc set behind a travertine throne. The pleasure of making things is unsurpassed.

The stone is cut by precision water jet that works like a laser, and is inlaid by specialists. It is very exciting watching a prehistoric material being worked in such an advanced way, and the results are beautiful. We also cut precise fluidly curved steps based on contour lines. I don't think this kind of cutting would have been possible before the water laser jet was invented.

Laser cutting was also used for the pavilion I created for the Chelsea Flower Show centenary for Prince Harry, this time using very strong birch plywood. I wanted to make a rotunda evocative of the shape of primitive houses. The original rondavel dwelling is essentially a timber frame clad in mud that dries in the sun and bakes and is then thatched. They have existed across many cultures and for many thousands of years. I wanted to make this rudimentary structure using all the technology that we have at our fingertips today. The birch ply is a technical timber – not simply cut from a tree but sliced like a veneer and laminated together into a very strong product. It is also environmentally friendly, as birch grow fast and there is very little waste. I combined this with CAD, Rhino modelling skills, 3D laser printing and laser cutting. The rondavel was very high-tech and very beautiful, with an open lens to the sky within it. Our craftsmanship skills have changed beyond recognition in recent years as the technology has developed.

Art and sculpture
An essay in caution

Art has to be handled with great care outside. Too much can leave a garden feeling overstuffed and visually confusing. I cut my teeth early by working for the Henry Moore Foundation, based at his old house at Perry Green, Hertfordshire. I wasn't employed to place art, of course, but I learned a great deal by discussing it with the curator, Moore's old assistant David Mitchinson. Admittedly all the work here is by the same artist, and that helps, but it is positioned in an honest way among Moore's old farm buildings and in sheep fields and somehow manages to capture the spirit of a man working, rather than someone posing work for effect. I liked that aspect of it.

In Scotland I inherited a large collection of sculpture to place. It was too much. We winnowed it down to a very few pieces, as even with thousands of acres to play with, it was easy for the place to feel cluttered. I ended up siting an Antony Gormley figure in a pine forest gazing towards the loch. The Gormley sculptures are readily recognizable and often seen in groups, so I felt it juxtaposed nicely with the grouping of the tree trunks. Marina Abramovic came over to help me understand one of her pieces and we had a hilarious few days shinning up and down mountains as we tried to situate a piece of her work. In the end we agreed it didn't really work and it went elsewhere. Art is mercurial stuff. It is very important to feel that it adds something meaningful to a garden, otherwise it runs the danger of becoming decorative, and that's a thing I don't care for. I'm just not interested in decoration.

It's a moot point whether landscape design itself is art or not. I feel the balance between the landscape and the chosen art has to be calibrated sensitively.

In Scotland during the restoration we unearthed this beautiful sculpture, *Scottish Orpheus,* by Hew Lorimer, which the original owner, Sir John Stirling-Maxwell, had commissioned for his house (ABOVE). It is a poignant piece and sits quietly overlooking the loch, surrounded by flowers, completely congruent to the location.

This was an exhibition piece made for the Jardins des Tuileries in Paris (LEFT). It was, in some respects, a prototype of a technique I was interested in trying, using moulding and casting.

Antony Gormley's *Here and Here, 2001* found a poignant home in the trees adjacent to the seized-up winch from the old paddle steamer that used to bring visitors to the lodge (OPPOSITE). I left the trees dense to increase the isolation.

Raw and sensitive landscape
healing the rift

LAIKIPIA, KENYA

————

The aim here was to blend a new building into the landscape as though it had always been there, hunkered down and all but invisible. The countryside here in the Kenyan Rift Valley is magical and home to the increasingly threatened black rhino. Our project forms part of a rhino conservancy plan spanning several large estates. Harmonizing with the environment is writ large here and the landscaping and architecture are complicit within it.

The early sketches contain all the ingredients that then filter through to the end result. The landscape developed well from the sketch design. I instigated a great deal more contouring and reshaping of the land as the power of the rains became apparent. We also pulled the wild bush planting tight to the walls and made the house really intimate within it. The courtyard, after many subsequent discussions, returned to the original drawing. These discussions are always invaluable and the sketches are the steady pulse of the original thinking.

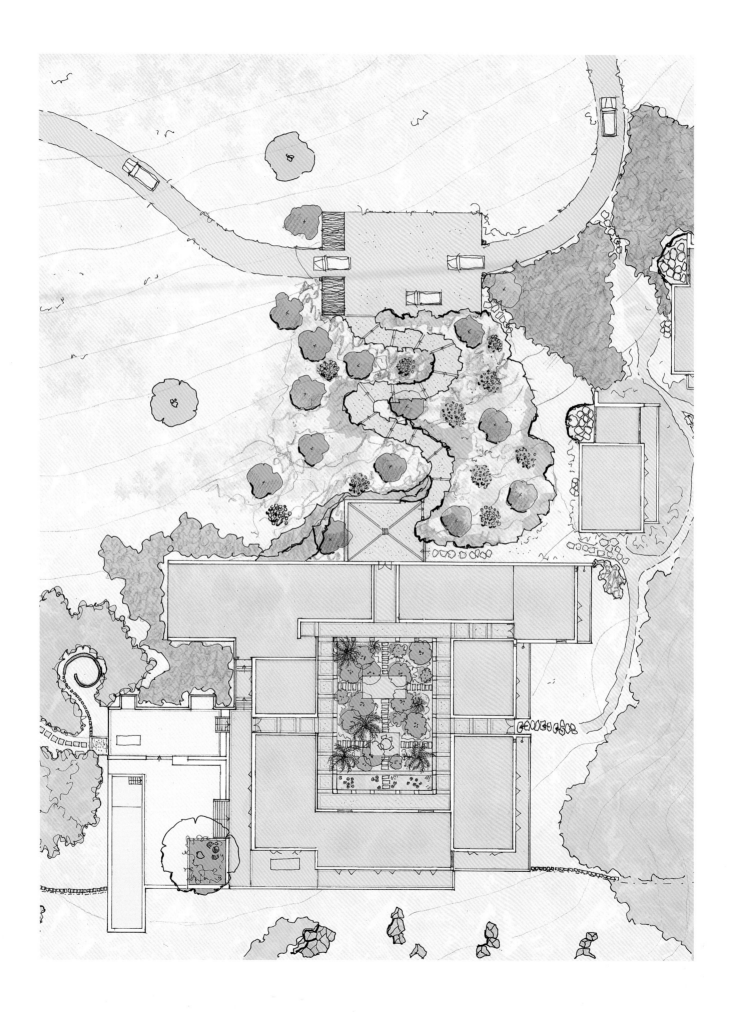

The architect, Alex Michaelis, is an old friend of many years and projects standing and we understand each other easily, so found it effortless to blend the feel of the hard landscaping with the house design. We are both half-French, so the language of hill villages, scarce water and monastic living is in our veins. Making a project like this work well is dependent on creating a local team of like-minded people who can understand and carry out the vision. I was very lucky to meet Michael Dyer, who heads up the conservancy, and drill him for locally appropriate information. We flew in his rickety Cessna over the local estates and I could see the devastating effect of erosion from overgrazing and lack of water. I ended up with a dream team. Llewellyn Dyer, a young Kenyan permaculture farmer, became my chief of staff and helped execute the scheme in tandem with running his farm. Ben Jackson created the hard landscape. He speaks fluent Swahili and is preternaturally good with many idioms of building. We would discuss details, he would translate them into Swahili and the local guys would fly into action. I needed the help on the ground – at one point we had 450 people working for us. The craftsmanship was beautiful.

The gardens are modest in relation to the wider landscaping. They are centred in the internal courtyard and beside the beautiful infinity pool that sits on the 'elephant ha-ha' designed to keep the humans safe. The terraces sit above the landscape and allow a ringside seat to all the passing animals.

The courtyard is calm, still and completely protected. Here I used water in a large pool and in pots to cool the space. Using variants of native plants makes a gentle mix of planting, and growing at almost visible speed are three thorny yellow fever trees that will create shade and texture as they emerge from the colonnaded space.

Blending together the people, the materials and the planting with the wider ethos of the conservancy and its overarching responsibility for protecting and caring for nature made this an extremely satisfying process.

The materials available to us were all local. I decided to use stone in various forms, and chose a smooth site-finished terrazzo in this lovely pale creamy colour for around the pool (PAGE 142). It all tones in beautifully with the surrounding landscape because it is made from it. Amorphous beds are cast directly into the terrazzo and make sheltered places to hang out (OPPOSITE ABOVE). I outcropped a few big boulders into them for texture and as a reminder of the rock-strewn landscape beyond the house. In the courtyard a quiet mixture of pennisetum, westringia and the native African black olive sit well with the pale Meru stone walls (PAGE 143).

Having needle-shaped leaves certainly helps conserve water and makes the westringia, rosemary and erigeron happy bedfellows (BELOW). Our client, right at the very beginning of the work, saved a venerable black olive as the site was being cleared (PAGES 140–41). The pleasure of lying beneath it as the pool juts out into the wild is a sumptuous feeling. It's not uncommon for an elephant's trunk to appear over the end of the pool. Water is for sharing.

The dead cedars that litter the landscape become effortlessly sculptural within the courtyard (RIGHT). I'm happy if they stay and become hosts for the climbers and perches for the birds.

Here is the elephant ha-ha bathed in evening light, showing all the millions of clumps of wild tussock grass we planted to stabilize the earth after the turmoil of building (PAGE 146).

I found the five vast pots on a nursery visit and persuaded the owner to sell them to us complete with their little cream water lilies ( ). In the middle of the dry landscape they are tiny miracles of life. Myriad birds visit them each day and the dragonflies are never far away.

Rooting

And so to plants, the subject that makes *bosoms heave and hearts swell*. All the months of machinery, mud and noise melt away into soft colours and birdsong in scented evening air. Yet ornamental planting is nature at her most mercurial. Understanding her tricks and seductions is essential for a happy garden. Hard work, trial and constant error and discussions with fellow gardeners is how good plant knowledge evolves. That knowledge is then constantly tested, as making plants combine well requires patience, skill and serendipity.

The gardener is the garden

There is no avoiding the fact. Plants are all about hard physical work. The majority of activities relating to plants and planting involve constant and sometimes back-breaking effort. If you want to be seduced by the subject, then just look at the pictures and stop reading! Gardeners, those of us who love gardening, are normally to be found face down presenting their posteriors to the world as they rummage around muttering into a border. We fall easily into intense coded conversations with others of our ilk that leave non-gardeners bewildered. One of the chicest women I know, America's great landscape architect Andrea Cochran, says she spends days on end at home in her vegetable garden, her battered trousers held up by bailer twine and not a thought for what she looks like. There is no absorption as profound as gardening. It is a form of transcendentalism. Garden admirers, on the other hand, are to be found genteelly dressed strolling slowly and admiringly through the afore-mentioned sumptuous borders.

I work like a carthorse in the garden. Born in the Chinese year of the ox, I expect I have no choice. I remember when I started out as a garden designer the terrifying figure of Mary Keen swept down upon me at the Chelsea Flower Show. She grabbed my hands hard by the wrists and examined them wordlessly. She flung them down. 'Good,' she said, 'you actually garden. You're all right.' We have liked each other ever since. Unless you garden it is quite difficult to make reliable gardens for others. It is essential to be able to understand the man-hours it will take to manage and maintain things. Temple Guiting, with its eighteen garden rooms, fourteen acres of garden and two sizeable vegetable gardens, is gardened part-time by Marion Jones, an impressive young Welsh woman. She has help with mowing and topiary clipping but everything else she does herself. I designed the garden to be self-managing and that doesn't mean no work at all – it just means it is focused, intelligent and cognizant of the person who will garden it. The gardener must be considered as integral to the design. My dear, departed friend Ian Kirby always said, 'The gardener is the garden' and it is the truth.

I wanted this border to be exuberant (PREVIOUS PAGES). It gets taller and wilder as the season progresses, tamed by the clipped forms of the *Quercus ilex* and illuminated for months with *Rosa* x *odorata* 'Mutabilis'.

This little garden bakes in south-facing heat, amplified by the enclosure, and the plants need to accommodate this (ABOVE). *Vitis coignetiae* is very much at home on the walls and blends well with the lavenders and *Elaeagnus* 'Quicksilver'.

I loved making these long walk borders (OPPOSITE). The yew columns march down as far as the barn and the *Quercus ilex*, where the tempo changes and the planting loosens. Viburnums, roses and philadelphus bolster the *Campanula lactiflora* 'Loddon Anna' and tumbling herbaceous plants all in shades of blue and white.

Soil
Mulch is magic

Let's get stuck in! This is the good bit. Finally, the building work is done and the planting can begin. Only, hold your horses, we aren't planting anything until the soil is sorted out.

Good soil has been my Holy Grail for as many years as I can remember. I have been gardening London clay for so long I almost lost my faith. It is enough to test the commitment of any gardener, as clay is so horrible to work. It seemed it was in workable condition for only a few miraculous weeks a year when it wasn't either baked to rock hardness with inch-wide cracks or a sullen stolid immoveable mass of damp misery. Tens of years' worth of manure and grit were swallowed up by it and it remained unyielding. London clay is a law unto itself. Inevitably the plants I most admire enjoy chalk or lovely dry friable limy soil. Irises detest the morosely clammy clay with its legions of slugs. Persistently I grew them and persistently the slugs would chomp through the neck of the stem below the bud like Monsieur Guillotin on a good day. Off with their heads! In desperation I relandscaped the garden specifically to dig out the clay and import good soil. *Et voilà!* Irises in full and glorious flower, albeit only for ten days a year.

I'm lucky enough to also have a garden out of London, where the soil is miraculously good, light, sandy, warm and sweet. Things grow like magic beans, my back doesn't ache and every day is a salad day. Generally, though, I am pragmatic about soil preparation, as replacing soil is not possible or appropriate in most cases. More often than not we set about improving it. It is easy to analyse topsoil. If it is moist and rolls into a ball in your fingers, then it is clay. Sand is self-evident, and the rest can be chalk, good loam or peat or stony schist.

All soils are improved by mulching. It holds the moisture beneath its blanket and opens up the top layer to oxygen and life. It also helps stop erosion. Spreading a thick layer over beautifully cleared soil in autumn is very satisfying. In my planting schemes there are areas where I try to persuade people not to clear up every leaf, but leave them to form a natural mat over the soil and let the worms do their work. Regular mulching reduces the need to dig and cuts down on labour. Good soil is a reward beyond words.

In wilder areas, if plants can be left to become self-mulching, then leave them in peace.

This is the tumultuous conclusion to the long walk seen on page 153, where it relaxes and spreads out, blurring with the natural surroundings (PREVIOUS PAGES). *Rosa californica* 'Plena' in the background supports waves of fennels, lavender, irises and salvias. The dry ground tempers the unruly behaviour of the valerian, with *Rosa* x *odorata* 'Pallida' (syn. 'Old Blush') playing to the crowd in front.

Rosa Iceberg ('Korbin') hedges are a bold move (OPPOSITE). They slice across the garden and brighten the woodland backdrop. Such great plants – flowering without cease and obligingly good looking and healthy. Heavy mulching is necessary on thin chalk soil.

This low wall needs thoughtful planting, nothing too uncontrollable (LEFT). I chose *Stipa calamagrostis* on the right of the gate and *Salvia* x *superba* to the left. *Vitis coignetiae* drapes nonchalantly behind.

My garden is on sand so drains like a sieve and is mulched, broadly speaking, with wild oregano (BELOW). Everything else just blasts up through it and it seems uncomplaining from the first bulbs to the last asters.

Structuring and layering planting
How it works

I have a belt-and-braces method for creating a planting plan. Planting is extremely difficult to visualize, as it is a four-dimensional puzzle. Knowing your plants is important. Failure is the bedfellow of ignorance, and as gardens are judged on their planting, it is pretty essential to get it to function adequately. It can be worth writing the critical plant facts – heights, flowering times, die-back period – on bits of paper and shuffle them round your desk. This way it's easy to see the rudiments of their performance and avoid obvious disasters. I taught myself by always following this system. Start with your shrubby backbone and build from there. Confidence grows quickly from this point, and having a structure to fall back on is helpful even now. Herbaceous plants have very varied structural natures and it is good to get to grips with friends and enemies who will help or hinder your borders. Using annuals to plug unforgiving gaps is also useful if you have access to them or can grow your own. They deserve a comeback.

I have a 'Salome's veils' approach to layering planting. It is important that there is enough airiness to allow each layer to suggest the next, but without giving the game away entirely.

My first paid garden design! Running water in the mill leet on one side and an orchard on the other. This little garden was carved from a bit of farmland and had never been cultivated. I didn't want to obscure the countryside or create a martyrdom of weeding on the bank, so I sketched the image from the top floor of the mill to help me ascertain the heights of the shrubbery (LEFT). Conclusion – nothing bigger than an elder.

This was my first proper planting design made flesh (OPPOSITE). It feels like I drew it with my tongue stuck out in concentration! I like it and it amuses me how stiffly I pooled and layered the plants. But it is important to learn, and learn I did. And this photograph by Andrew Lawson launched my career. Thank you, Andrew!

Trees
Folk heroes

Starting at the top of the planting plan pyramid are trees – it is very important to scale them to the location and think ahead twenty, thirty years and more. In smaller gardens I tend to use fruit trees, or containable trees such as *Catalpa* x *erubescens* that can be hard-pruned. Amelanchiers and the smaller maples work – *Acer griseum* is good and so too is *Cercis siliquastrum*. Try to smother each season with something good to enjoy: flowers, changing foliage colour, interesting bark and perhaps fruit or seed pods. A well-chosen tree will do all of this in a small space and earn its keep well. In parkland, of course, it's possible to plant much larger trees and, again, I urge consideration of planting distances between trees. Avenue trees must be planted 10m (39 feet) apart. No large tree will enjoy being planted closer, and in a few years the mistake becomes obvious as the crowns collide and the trees look miserable.

A lot of trees these days are cloned in production, so it is worth knowing at the outset whether you are buying cloned or seed-grown trees. It makes a difference to the ultimate character of the plant. I prefer trees not to be uniform, but that is a personal choice.

Then, of course, there are the pleached and espaliered trees. Lime, pear, hornbeam, apple and liquidambar are the usual suspects for me. A Frenchman told me that all pleached and espaliered trees are unfashionable. I told the Frenchman I was unmoved by fashion. They are too good a building block to worry about what they are wearing. I use box heads or espaliers a lot – I also use espaliered screens where space is limited. I think it was probably a seminal visit to the baroque Palace of Het Loo in the Netherlands that got me started. The amazing arched hornbeam tunnel was quite an inspiration. Trees are malleable enough to be formed to create architecture.

Here is the Urban Glamour Wood that became an RIBA prizewinner and a shoot location for many well-known fashionistas (OPPOSITE). A few humble *Betula pendula* and some tousled sexy planting are all it took.

This is an entirely constructed scene (ABOVE). I bought a redundant fruit research station in Belgium. These are special hazelnut varieties that had been pruned beautifully for propagation. Now retired from active service and bedded into long grass, they've never been happier.

These lovely old boys were lost among overgrown shrubs, so I hoicked them all out and restored the sward (ABOVE). The little bridge over the ha-ha is possible now we no longer graze this area. The grazing line on the canopies will now gradually drop without the attention of the deer.

I make no claim here other than the surprise and delight of coming across a vast grove of these now wild rhododendron, collected and planted in the Highlands by Sir John Stirling-Maxwell some 135 years ago (LEFT). I wish he could see it as he must have imagined it.

I have an addiction to crack willow and plant them whenever I can near water (OPPOSITE). I think my love stems from the really ancient ones that lined the river where I grew up. I'm from Shakespeare country, and they felt old enough for him to have known them. They're as useful as they are characterful.

Topiary
Shape shifters

Topiary is essential to many of my gardens. It is a very necessary anchor in loose herbaceous plantings, as it holds the eye as firmly as a building or a wall. I favour beech and yew and, if it's warm enough, myrtle and bay. I'm keeping away from box until the terrible blight that afflicts it calms down — if it ever does. I love box as a wild shrub so am happy with *Buxus sempervirens* 'Rotundifolia' left to grown large and beautiful. Box is a terrible loss to the topiarist but I do think we have to accept it as a fact and move on. There are plenty of things that will take a good shaping. Westringia is pretty if you need silvery leaves. And, of course, osmanthus takes a good prune after flowering, and smells beautiful in flower. I've only tried *Ilex crenata* once and it defoliated on me, so I've left it in peace since then.

Staggered sizes and mixed blocks of yew and beech create a crenellated hedge or semi-maze along a problematic boundary (OPPOSITE). They change colour beautifully in autumn and maintain the contrast through the winter months when it is needed. By the house I used the tree *Robinia pseudoacacia* as a soft airy adjunct to all the structural planting.

My garden in London benefits from the little box cubes and the dumpy cloud hedge at the back (ABOVE). They stop the planting flopping onto the path between the terraces.

Topiary is so immensely useful. Brimming with character, it can fasten the layers of a garden and balance different textures.

This garden is filled with huge bulks of loosely clipped *Buxus sempervirens*, forming partitions between spaces (ABOVE). On the boundary of the garden I used *Buxus sempervirens* 'Rotundifolia', which is reaching around 2.5m (8 feet). Topiary is excellent for nesting birds as well as for its visual uses.

Texturally I wanted some evergreen bulk to balance the ephemeral *Rosa laevigata* and *Rosa* 'New Dawn' and the contorted mulberry (LEFT).

This is the mother of all topiary: a forest of wild *Buxus sempervirens* at home in France (OPPOSITE). Heaven only knows how old it is. It's like being lost in an enchanted kingdom, with the soft fairy mosses hanging from the trunks and the cool moss-covered rocks and ferns underfoot.

Shrubs
Bring back shrubberies

Below the trees come the shrubs. They haven't been very fashionable in recent years, with gardening being in the thrall of the perennial and meadow movements. They certainly earn their keep in my world, creating the all-important middle layer. They give a backdrop to the floral border. Pragmatically they offer flowers, scent, autumn colour, nesting sites for birds, food and lodging for insects and attractive winter structure. I adore viburnums, hydrangeas, tree peonies and, to my own great surprise, rhododendrons. Rhododendrons, where the soil suits them, can be planted into the most magnificently harmonious groves like no other plant. In Scotland we discovered hundreds of them hidden away on a spruce-covered hillside and forgotten since their Victorian collector brought them back from the Himalayas and set about re-creating that landscape. The plants had grown to immense size and there, in their moistly dripping Highland haven, they flourished in peace (see page 162 for the evidence). Happy rhododendrons don't flower very much and this forever exorcized my horror of them that originated from the dumpy, gaudy plantations I remember as a child on visits to a distant cousin. I am fond of any shrub that drips romance and carries us through the bleaker seasons with their blurry outlines shrouded in mists.

 Often the gardens I make are quite large, so I would be lost without shrubberies. It is vital to take up space, literally waste space, and give that intermediate tier to a garden, and shrubs are so very giving in this. You do need to care for both layers though. The trees need thinning to give light to the shrubbery below. 'Neglect and die', if I might paraphrase P. W. Botha.

Batty Langley's account in 1728 of the 'Manner of Disposing and Planting Flowering Shrubs' appeared in his ground-breaking book *New Principles of Gardening*. His descriptions are sufficient even to this day for understanding how best to dispose shrubberies and create wildernesses.

The palette of plants for this semi-wild city
garden in New York needed to be chic and gentle
(OPPOSITE). I used big banks of *Hydrangea
quercifolia*. It is well known and that doesn't
matter – it loves living here and thrives below
the forest oak canopy.

Nothing but shrubs will do here (ABOVE).
The ground is covered with the exquisite little
Cornus canadensis, and then layers of hydrangea,
viburnum and *Magnolia virginiana* build up the
levels into the canopies of the oaks and pines.

Climbing plants
Agility and grace – the athletes

Once the tree and shrub layers are clarified on a plan, I move next to the climbers. Vines, roses, wisterias, clematis, jasmines and all manner of exotica can be used. Every region of the world has its party piece and it's worth using them. Plants that are popular are popular for a reason, so don't be too clever – just plant them and enjoy. The note of caution I'd sound is that most climbers do need someone competent to look after them. An unwieldy mess ensues without good pruning and training, and you end up needing binoculars to see the flowers at the top while being greeted with a horror of bald stems at the base. However, if this obstacle can be surmounted, then I advocate using them lavishly. Not everyone can do as Dame Miriam Rothschild did and smother the entire house, but an organized close second is worth considering. I think carefully about what I'm planting onto. Some houses either can't take, or don't need, a lot of climbers. Sometimes it's nicer to plant shrubs in front of a façade if the house is decorative enough without needing more.

A pergola or frame designed expressly for climbers is invaluable. Decoratively it can unite disparate parts of a garden, and the plants benefit from plenty of air and sun, so they grow beautifully and strongly.

We found vines of a large size, and in some cases quite loaded with grapes; we also found an abundance of roses, which appeared to be like those of Castile.

—JUNIPERO SERRA

The most modest of climbers, and yet the most giving (ABOVE). These sweet peas were planted fairly thoughtlessly and yet scented the house all summer. I love them.

Rosa 'Paul's Scarlet Climber' is a tremendous rose (OPPOSITE). It's not scented, yet who cares as it flowers without end and is obligingly healthy and strong. Paired with a well-pruned grape-vine of indistinct parentage, it enhances rather than overpowers the house.

Rose gardens
The throbbing heart

Cy Twombly hated roses. I'm amazed to find his loathing of them so well recorded! Finding time in his all-consuming artistic life to make his feelings known means the feeling must have run deep. I love roses. Every garden I have ever made has been vastly enriched by their presence. The air is heavy with their perfume. Bees bumble lazily from flower to flower. 'Come into the garden, Cy, you just don't know what you are missing.'

I only love certain types of roses though. For easy opulence and lack of disease I tend to go for the Bourbons. I planted an entire flint wall with 'Honorine de Brabant' and, in the capable secateurs of the gardener, it flowered like the sort of wall of roses you tend to see in books. It just needed lavender at its feet, so that's what I gave it. In my experience the Bourbons don't need a lot of messing about with. Plant them into fantastically well-prepared soil, having first root- and top-pruned them quite hard, and leave them to it. I prune hard in the first year to stop them rocking and then not much after that. I rather like their big unwieldy shapes. For something neater I love the Portland 'Comte de Chambord'. Having no fear of pink I find it can be the base note of some fairly exciting colour combinations, and it smells beautiful.

I'm veering back towards the frowned-upon Hybrid Teas. Much maligned in the UK due to overenthusiastic municipal planting forty-odd years ago, they are thought of pejoratively as 'granddad' flowers. A full load was wrongly delivered recently by an unscrupulous trader and we planted them, thinking they would fill an empty summer until the right ones turned up bare-rooted in the autumn. I was astonished by the vigorous purple shoots, the scent and the really rather nice foliage – planted in one of my looser schemes they came into their own and I decided to keep them. Gardening is all about serendipitous accidents, so there's no point being too uptight about mistakes. My favourite Hybrid Tea is 'Mrs Oakley Fisher'. It is very tasteful, though, with slender flame buds opening to a single apricot rose. Christopher Lloyd once chastised me, saying my choices of plants were 'rather too tasteful'. It's a recrimination I can live with. Perhaps one of the best climbing Hybrid Teas is 'Lady Hillingdon'– a rather wonderful heavy apricot-yellow rose that hangs its head down shyly. Lady Hillingdon was the wife of an Indian Viceroy and is reputedly the originator of the phrase, 'I close my eyes, open my legs, lie back and think of England', as she heard her husband coming up the stairs. Not a bed of roses for her then!

Hybrid Tea roses are due a renaissance and I'm happy to be heading it. I used *Rosa* A Whiter Shade of Pale in this mix (ABOVE). I love the song and I love the rose.

A strong clear pink is essential in a garden and, to stop it looking too much like a girlie bedroom, I weight it down with serious magenta and navy, such as these *Lychnis coronaria* and deep blue *Campanula* 'Kent Belle' (OPPOSITE). This is *Rosa* 'Comte de Chambord', planted in vast quantities.

This is the kind of wall I dream of (PREVIOUS PAGES)! It probably once had a vast glasshouse built on it, hence the lumps of oak all through it. Now it looks like a work of art. I didn't want to swamp it, so chose the spare frame of climbing *Rosa* The Pilgrim from David Austin. The flowers are large enough and constant enough to register against the stunning stonework.

Dear Lady Hillingdon. Here she is immortalized in the most beautiful climbing rose, created in 1917 (OVERLEAF). I hope the eponymous rose and the wedding gift of Overstrand Hall, one of Lutyens' best houses, diminished her horror of her husband's feet creaking upstairs towards her!

Flowers and subshrubs
The complicated bit

The blending and weaving of herbaceous plants is possibly the trickiest part of a garden. It is the mutable element that brings both sublime joy and unutterable sorrow and is, I think, akin to making music in its subtlety and complexity. Sigmund Freud observed that flowers engender a sense of peace, as they suffer neither from conflict or feelings. That said, Sigmund, you do have to give quite a bit of thought to the party guests or it could be a very unfulfilling event. Not every truism is true.

Technical understanding of plants and their vagaries will only take you so far when designing. At some point it is important to cut loose, take risks and fly. I don't know how much help can be given, as it is such a personal process – it is, after all, about creating a living painting.

My own approach is probably based in replicating matrices that are quite close to nature. I'm not a 'wild' gardener by any means, as I am far too organized for that, yet I like the plants in my schemes to get on with each other and coexist in a companionable way. I've developed my own style of blending herbaceous plants so that there is always something happening, even in a very restricted space and within a restricted palette. My gardens really have to work. I am giving people something with an evolutionary life and that is a responsibility and needs to be fully understood.

I work with a relatively pared-down plant palette that I know I can rely on to perform. Gardening at home for myself, I can try out all sorts of things and make it all up as I go along. That is completely permissible in a private arena, but for my work I need to be focused and more measured. Soil, orientation and space are considered well in advance. In one small London garden I think I used just six species, and the instruction was to keep them in equal balance. The garden was planted well over ten years ago and is still going strong – as plants tire, they are replaced. If one variety becomes too powerful, it can be split. Other times, as in Kenya, I wanted a much more complex solution, as the evolution of planting there is extremely rapid. The equatorial climate offers nonstop growth without discernible seasons. This planting needed to weave together and then balance into a toughed-out wilderness matrix. The intellectual process for this is more akin to creating a permaculture than a garden. The area is remote and wild and aesthetically there is a danger of it looking like a hotel if over-gardened in a traditional way. I'm not up for that! I do try to move things along a bit in my work.

Plumbago, named because 'plumbum' is Latin for lead (ABOVE). Pliny believed it cured lead poisoning, as the flowers are of a similar colour to the metal. I like it as a plant for interstices between grasses. It flowers well and is undemanding in heat.

Campanula 'Kent Belle' with *Papaver orientale* 'Patty's Plum' knitted together with the still emerging *Calamintha nepeta* (OVERLEAF LEFT). Glistening in the background are the buds of *Lilium martagon.* I use these plants often, as they make comfortable bedfellows and the colours are so sumptuous.

Frequently I'm happy with very little. Plants needs space in order to shine. This is *Knautia macedonica* but came up as a pale pink rather than the conventional magenta (OVERLEAF RIGHT). Enjoyably random.

Early summer in the Peacock Garden (BELOW). I enjoy the emerging rusty orange of *Eremurus* x *isabellinus* 'Cleopatra', knowing it will soon be in full swing with the crimson claret of *Cirsium rivulare* 'Atropurpureum'. When this garden gets cracking, the colours rival Christian Lacroix in his heyday.

An example of a good hardworking border exists at Temple Guiting in a very narrow bed 70m long and 1m deep (230 by 3 feet) that is filled with the espaliered hornbeams. (You can see it in its various seasonal guises on pages 193–947.) The trees are greedy for water. I keep them tightly espaliered so light gets to the border. The skill needed was to combine very tough herbaceous plants with the trees so the symbiotic competition worked. Know this – the beautiful peony *Paeonia lactiflora* 'Duchesse de Nemours' is a very tough old bird! Her looks belie her character. Combining her with cardoons, *Dianthus* 'Mrs Sinkins' – another *grande dame* who can hold her own – and lavenders, the border has chugged on for a remarkably long time. There isn't a grass in sight for reasons I will explain next. It is hard-core romantic herbaceousness and, guess what, people love it. Beauty changes how we feel, there is no doubt about it, and it is good.

Thank goodness for immigrants
in horticulture, or we would have
nothing to plant!

Grasses
Kissing the wind

Grasses were vital in the courtyard in Kenya (OPPOSITE). The landscape is open grassland and so the planting combination needed a variety of plants scattered through a backbone of grasses, as occurs naturally. Otherwise it would be like jam without toast – not very nice.

The roadside nurseries of Nairobi aren't big on labels so I don't know which pennisetum this is (BELOW). Is has the right diffuse non-colour necessary to bring together the planting.

After their rock'n'roll moment, grasses are settling into part of the rhythm of well-loved garden plants.

Grasses come next. I use them sparingly. Piet Oudolf is a good friend and I greatly admire his work, though my planting is very different. He is a genuinely original thinker and very much copied. Piet and his wife Anja are amazingly knowledgeable plants people and generous to a fault with that knowledge. The percentage of grass to herbaceous in Piet's schemes is probably a good deal less than popular perception gives us to remember. I just fact-checked that in his book and am correct. Grasses are extremely useful when used as an adjunct or a statement within a more varied collection of species. However I am cautious of inflicting too many grasses on a gardener, and here is why. In the first big garden I planted at The Menagerie, I used *Miscanthus sacchariflorus* to form a series of serpentine paths leading to a temple and also to the water's edge. I've always loved the feeling of being out of scale to my surroundings, and moving through the shimmering grass was a beautiful experience. This grass grows cheerfully to about 3m (10 feet) tall. And it did – it was very happy indeed. And then I had to look after it and garden it and try and hoick couch grass out of its congested stems. Couch grass is the 'dirty bomb' of gardening. In late winter, cutting the miscanthus back to ground level engendered the need to sing songs of the chain gangs to keep myself going; hard and bloody work. And I vowed I could never inflict large swathes of biomass on anyone ever again, however fabulous its swishing tresses. It was the moment that I understood that if I wanted to be a free expressionist, it would have to be in my own time, as that level of artistic excess is suited only to the solipsist!

My grasses of choice are the gentler ones. I use the panicums a fair bit, also *Calamagrostis* x *acutiflora* 'Karl Foerster' – even though people claim it's boring, it is very useful. I also like the smaller grasses, such as *Milium effusum* 'Aureum', which lights up shady spots and is never a pain. The stipas are also good, and I have a special place in my heart for the beautiful *Ampelodesmos mauritanicus*. Get to know the habit of the grass and use it accordingly. Better to have a few that really look good than cram them into the wrong spot. In my new garden I've just gleefully dug out all the horrible little blue festucas. I know for a fact that if I saw them in their native habitat, I'd love them, but in gardens they are static spotty runt among other free-flowing plants. So in essence I suggest investigating the natural growth pattern in the wild of the grasses you like, seeing if that look is what you are after and then mimicking it.

Ferns

A slow reveal

I definitely have Pteridomania. It's been untreated for a while, as I haven't really had access to a good place to build a proper fernery. I can't survive without my tree ferns and it broke my heart to leave a well-tended and enormous *Woodwardia radicans* with a friend, as they had the perfect conditions and I didn't – that was well over thirty years ago and the pain is as raw as ever. I was an odd teenager.

In our teens my best friend Ian Kirby had a flat in a vast old Victorian mansion that was semi-derelict. It was built in the faux Elizabethan style and was extremely picturesque. That saved it from being viewed as the untenable dump that it was. Ferns grew inside and out and mosses clustered on the damp maroon wool carpets. So taken were we with this colonization that we ornamented the toilet basin with collected moss and tree bark tied on with florists' wire. The flat had a vast old fernery built onto the room we used as a kitchen. It was a conservatory of sorts, with complex tufa rustication smothering the walls and a defunct watering system of old lead pipework. It would have been a technological marvel in its day and we set about repairing it with a will. Maidenhair fern liked it best, along with blechnums and aspleniums. Had we known about it, we would have used *Selaginella kraussiana* too, but we made do with the ubiquitous 'ferner's friend' *Soleirolia soleirolii*, or baby's tears. Hours were spent misting and fogging to keep it all drippingly happy.

I use ferns wherever I can in cool spaces. They do need the right conditions to thrive, so check carefully. There is nothing worse than watching plants suffer from the indifference of bad placement.

Everything I love about France is in my garden wall (ABOVE). The ferns have chosen to live here and no one has ever said they can't. It's a happy symbiosis.

I so enjoyed creating this garden (OVERLEAF). It's full of things I love: *Genista aetnensis*, *Dicksonia antarctica*, the delicious honey-scented spurge *Euphorbia mellifera* and *Astelia chathamica*, all woven into a matrix of grasses. What's not to love!

Currently there are well over 10,000 fern species alive and well on earth. Their enigmatic antiquity and stimulating way of unfurling their fronds make them indispensable.

In Scotland, happy in the unending soft rain is *Dryopteris wallichiana* (LEFT). The black hairy ribs of the leaves catch tiny drops of water and glisten beautifully. One of my favourite ferns, as its big and semi-evergreen.

One of my tree ferns at home bathed in early morning light (BELOW). I've got a little grove of them and although they'd much rather be in New Zealand they are making the best of it here. I water them daily with rainwater to keep them pliable.

Bulbs, corms and rhizomes
Joy division

How to make a garden happy? Plant loads of bulbs, and I mean loads. In the depths of winter, up pop the snowdrops, crocuses, the sheets of aconites and the anemones. Then hot on their frosty heels come the narcissi and hyacinths, muscari and scillas, then the bluebells, fritillaries and camassias. The tulips come in great fanfares and save you from thinking spring is but a damp squib with nothing to commend it after months of winter. A spring garden without tulips is a sorry sight. I'm especially fond of them, as our family crest is three flamed yellow tulips, bestowed by a cheerful King Christian IV of Denmark for reasons we will never know. We all know about tulipomania and it was justified and still is.

After tulips, the alliums – getting bored yet? No? Alliums of all colours and sizes are great in a garden, but try to avoid the mistake I saw recently of planting in a sheltered garden far too many *Nectaroscordum siculum*. They reek to high heaven and it does rather spoil the effect. Then the summer flowers: irises, crinums, nerines and lilies. Lilies have been ruined for me by the invasion of the revolting scarlet lily beetle, Lilioceris lilii. We are under constant siege from invading enemies that make life so frustrating. I am going to try again though and see what can be achieved, as life without lilies is a lesser life.

In the Middle East I've enjoyed discovering bulbs that create such a show over there in spring. They are so well adapted to the ferocious terrain and brutal sun and yet flower with grace and delicacy, and add so much to the planting schemes. There are so many good bulbs and corms it is impossible to list them, but suffice to say they earn their keep many times over as they take up so little space and give back so much.

With careful planning, there is a bulb for every month of the year, and the pleasure of them is immeasurable.

Allium hollandicum 'Purple Sensation' lives up to its name and I plant them in thousands every year. Despite their ubiquity I haven't a bad word to say about them – I just plant some more.

At the other end of the spectrum is this delicate Turkish species tulip, *Tulipa acuminata* (OPPOSITE). It is surprisingly versatile and creates wonderful displays if it can naturalize. I'm having another go now I've moved to a garden with better soil for it.

This orchid is in one of the damp meadows at home in France (LEFT). I'm not certain but think it's *Orchis purpurea*, the lady orchid. They appear in sheets with the strange tasselled *Muscari* and are extremely ornamental.

One of the nameless wild *Iris germanica* that thrive at the base of the walls of my house in France (BELOW). Their rhizomes bake in the heat of the summer.

This is part of a colony of *Dactylorhiza* that suddenly appeared in my flowery mead this year (BOTTOM). Patience rewarded.

Lilium regale is such a good doer and seems to deal with the dreaded lily beetle well enough for me to keep planting it (OPPOSITE). Garden borders need incursions from the glam squad from time to time.

Orchids require patience. Plant them and then go and concentrate on other things for a few years and let them surprise you.

Plant groupings
Getting the party started

A good planting combination is a happy party of not too many guests who all allow each other time and space to express themselves. We now have the hierarchy of the plants and the layering, and then it falls to making bewitching combinations that work for a space. Drawing out planting plans is the best thing and I still draw them by plant diameter. I make my list following the hierarchy and then I plan them out. I then trawl through and see what the behaviour is like – there is nothing worse than planning something, as I once did with *Euphorbia griffithii* 'Fireglow', and then not realizing that it leaves a hole a yard across.

I like my gardens to settle into an easy compatibility of plants and give effortlessly charming results. I'm flatteringly told that my gardens are all about planting. Quite a lot has been written about me to that effect by people who don't know me. My own view is that they are all about good planning and structure and then that is overlaid with well-thought-out planting. Temple Guiting looks incredibly plant-driven, but it has very few mixed borders in relation to its size. I just used plants that sing out lustily the joy of summer. I do that almost criminal thing of making the gardens pretty, because pretty makes us happy.

Hand-drawing planting plans helps me understand the layering and seasonal movement. I think the complexity of a planting plan is often misunderstood.

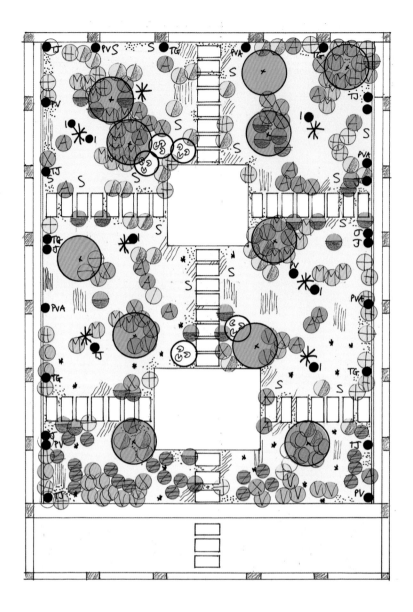

Soon the stepping stones in the courtyard will disappear in a tide of planting. (ABOVE AND OPPOSITE ABOVE) Shooting through this scheme are spots of rich reds and oranges that also appear fleetingly in the natural landscape.

The joy of good planting is intoxicating – with no awful side effects. The muted slatey grey blue of the plumbago offsets well with the subtle colour shifts in the garden (OPPOSITE LEFT).

How to grow without being eaten? Get yourself some thorns like this acacia (OPPOSITE RIGHT).

By choosing good bedfellows a garden will semi-naturalize. Going back to my roots in France, I observed how plants in nature grow into self-moderating and companionable groups, and I can't reiterate enough how important it is to understand the rudiments of a genus and how it adapts to its location. I had neither the means nor the method to travel much when I was younger, so I read voraciously instead. The very best gardening books for me, other than those by Graham Stuart Thomas, were those by Roger Phillips and Martyn Rix, published by Macmillan. I have worn them out several times over, thumbing through and memorizing the habitat of the plants. In more recent years I have been able to travel and see things for myself, and this information is invaluable. There is no substitute for getting to know plants personally and learning their Latin names. Latin is a practical language and holds a lot of the relevant information about the character of the plant within it — very useful shorthand for remembering who your friends are and what they like.

The main canal garden border at Temple Guiting in June, flowering beneath slimly espaliered hornbeams (PREVIOUS PAGES). I cut them slim for maximum light. Even before they leaf up, the hornbeam espaliers are good architectural screens (OPPOSITE ABOVE). Cardoons are controlled by the power of the trees. The same border in late April shows why tulip planting is so vital for the early months (BELOW). By late May the beds are getting going and the hornbeams are fully leafed up and doing their job beautifully (OPPOSITE BELOW).

The planting plan tells you very specifically how many plants are needed, as they accurately show the final plant diameter (OPPOSITE LEFT).

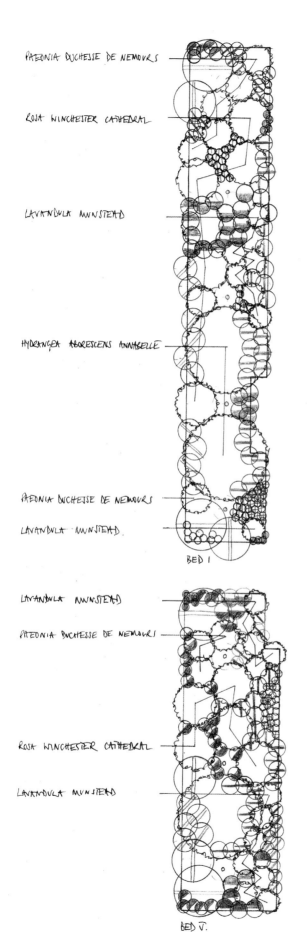

PAEONIA DUCHESSE DE NEMOURS

ROSA WINCHESTER CATHEDRAL

LAVANDULA MUNSTEAD

HYDRANGEA ARBORESCENS ANNABELLE

PAEONIA DUCHESSE DE NEMOURS

LAVANDULA MUNSTEAD.

BED 1

LAVANDULA MUNSTEAD

PAEONIA DUCHESSE DE NEMOURS

ROSA WINCHESTER CATHEDRAL

LAVANDULA MUNSTEAD

BED V.

The kitchen door
Food in the garden

If you could show the cabbage that I planted with my own hands to your emperor, he definitely wouldn't dare suggest that I replace the peace and happiness of this place with the storms of a never satisfied greed. – DIOCLETIAN

There has to be food in a garden. Diocletian was right. There is no greater sense of achievement than that of collecting herbs, fruit and vegetables from your garden. I always plant something edible, however lowly, such as alpine strawberries, in my gardens – if the humans don't get them, then the birds and mini mammals will. It is a constant battle against our proliferating pests, though. I always factor in a practical space for growing vegetables and fruit. I like raised beds that aren't too big and stick to a tried and trusted method of making them out of green oak. However the cultivation rests with the garden owner. Very little space is required to feed a family. I was on the train once when a young guy started going crazy as we pulled into London. He ran up and down the carriage making strange anxious grunts as he looked out of the window. Looking at me, he said, in anguished tones, 'Magpies? Why doesn't anyone kill them? We kill them on the farm.' He still lives with the urgent imperative of being self-sustaining, whereas most of us don't.

One of two of our vegetable patches at Temple Guiting (OPPOSITE). They started off modestly and now supply a famous restaurant in central London with fresh produce and sweet peas.

We dug up the lawns and put in vegetable beds while returning everything else to managed wilderness in the anti-garden (BELOW). There is no solace like a freshly pulled radish!

Meadows

Love in the long grass

Meadows are part of a farming cycle of grazing and haymaking. Our pastoralist forebears recognized thousands of years ago that using grazing animals can be an efficient way of harnessing otherwise unusable resources like grass. The species count in a proper old meadow is intense.

A meadow in a garden is, as far as I am concerned, just an element of gardening. Being pedantic about the etymology, 'meadow' means land covered in grass that is mown for hay. Hay is animal fodder. A 'meadow-y' area of long grass, like the millefleurs of medieval tapestries, studded with other flowers and in a garden setting, is nevertheless valuable and attractive. It becomes a pretty interstice between other elements. If space permits, I will add a flowery mead, both for all the life it supports and for aesthetic purposes – a garden equivalent of a sorbet.

A year earlier this had been a pristine manicured striped lawn (BELOW). It was miraculous to see how it metamorphosed into this hummocky bee-filled gentleness.

My little orchard mead at home, alive with oxeye daisy, clover and orchids (OPPOSITE). It is also hosting some very fine plums and apples. On the right is the start of the garden, and the tiny mown path is all that's needed to separate one mood from another.

In the anti-garden we allowed the grassland to develop with very little interference other than removing tree saplings (OVERLEAF). It is poetic. Feet on a regular route to the greenhouse beat through the tiny path.

The nut trees in the nuttery slowly strip fertility from the soil and allow the grassland to become more species-rich (ABOVE). The rougher textures of the land help return the house to its bucolic Tudor roots.

Plantago lanceolata, or ribbed plantain, is a very common meadow herb and has been known across northern Europe since Neolithic times (OPPOSITE). It is made immortal to me in Albrecht Dürer's much loved painting of turf.

Graziers have known for thousands of years that by rearing herbivorous animals they can utilize and improve open grassland. Grass is an otherwise unusable resource.

Hedges
Living on the hedge

Native hedgerows when well managed are filled with food and practicality. They form protective boundaries and hum with sustaining resources of food and fuel. The basic structure of a hedge is as follows. It has intermittent tall trees, such as oak, field maple, sweet chestnut and ash, then below a base of several flowering and nectar-rich shrubby plants, often including hawthorn, hazel, spindle, cherry plum, wild cherry, wild apple and pear, viburnums, rowans, holly, sloes, bullace and elder – a very great deal of fruit. Twining and scrambling plants come next: dog roses and sweet briar, blackberries, honeysuckles, hops, old man's beard and then not often seen but entirely appropriate are wild gooseberry, blackcurrant, raspberry and redcurrant, depending on location.

While not a traditional hedge, I tried to make the divisions in this garden as safe routes for wildlife using old gnarly pears and box (ABOVE). Food and shelter in abundance.

Hedges were frequently planted on banks so the resulting ditch would hold water and sustain all the smaller species at the base: primroses, wild strawberries, lady's bedstraw, hedge garlick, and chamomile and other herbs such as oregano and marjoram, with mint thriving in the damper areas. Also in the vicinity you might find wild asparagus, chicory, mallow, horseradish – the list goes on and on. I once counted up to 129 useful species in a hedge and its close neighbourhood. Hedges are so good for wildlife that 130 priority species in the UK Biodiversity Action Plan are associated with them. I chose to demonstrate hedge laying in my first foray into the Chelsea Flower Show on behalf of HRH Prince Charles. He is extremely skilled at it. We managed to lay a hawthorn hedge in full flower.

The uses derived from a hedge are diverse. Principally they protect us from invaders or contain animals with their thorny density. I plant a hedge on every project as a matter of course. The tall trees were also used for building materials, furniture, cartwheels, tools, charcoal, firewood, smoking, tanning, fruit such as acorns for animal feed, or sweet chestnuts for human consumption, as well as dyes and fuel. From the hedgerow shrubs came fruit and nuts in abundance, as well as finer hardwoods such as spindle and holly for turning and making needles, boxes, skewers, pegs and lamp oil. Without hazel there would be no wattles for wattle and daub, or baskets or walking sticks or beanpoles or kindling or water divining. Hedges prevent soil erosion and capture pollutants from fertilizers and pesticides, store carbon and also provide homes for many creatures that feed on pests.

Of course, with the easy availability of internet shopping and a global economy that is clearly destined to be robust and long-lasting, we

Hedges are peculiarly British phenomena, although corrals and living vegetal structures exist across the world as defensive enclosures. All of these can be adapted and used decoratively and functionally in gardens.

This deceptively bucolic scene is actually my first ever design for the Chelsea Flower Show for HRH Prince Charles (BELOW). We lifted great lumps of the organic meadow in full flower from the field's home, Highgrove House. I used them to front the hawthorn hedge that we laid in full flower. In 2002 this wasn't at all in vogue and I think I appeared a bit of an oddity for doing it! How times change.

no longer need any of this stuff. We can simply enjoy the very pretty succession of blossom and fruit that the hedge affords. And the pastoral idyll brought to us by the near proximity of songbirds, various tits and greater horseshoe and Natterer's bats that use hedges as green 'commuter routes' for foraging and roosting.

The sheer quantity of flowering species in a hedge makes a rich resource for bees, and beekeeping was a natural part of the system. Hazel catkins are the earliest pollen source, shaking out their golden dust in February before we are even aware the year has begun. A by-product of this concentration of good things is the physical habitat for so many creatures that is produced. Apparently up to 284 species of insect live on an English oak tree, and around 324 species of lichen, not to mention all those that benefit from the rest of the hedge and all the birds, mammals and invertebrates that find comfort and safety in the dense thorny structure. Every home must have one.

Planting in tune with history
choral florae

———

My heart was in my mouth when I first saw this place in a state of terrible dilapidation. I had the spine-tingling feeling of having been here before. The house is ancient. It sits in the most exquisite little valley of the Windrush River, deep in the proper Cotswolds. It dawned on me. I had been here many times before when I was a child, as the eccentric owners kept llamas and peacocks and we would ride over to see them. What an opportunity it presented to an enthusiast like me to bring it back to life.

The assembly of buildings is original to the medieval farmstead that has existed here since the Domesday Book. This plan evolved based on historic research, returning many of the long-vanished walled enclosures to their original positions. My strategy was to then make a series of related and interconnected gardens – eighteen in all – that would have different colour senses. Conscious of Cotswold traditionalism, I wanted them to be sumptuous, gentle and timeless.

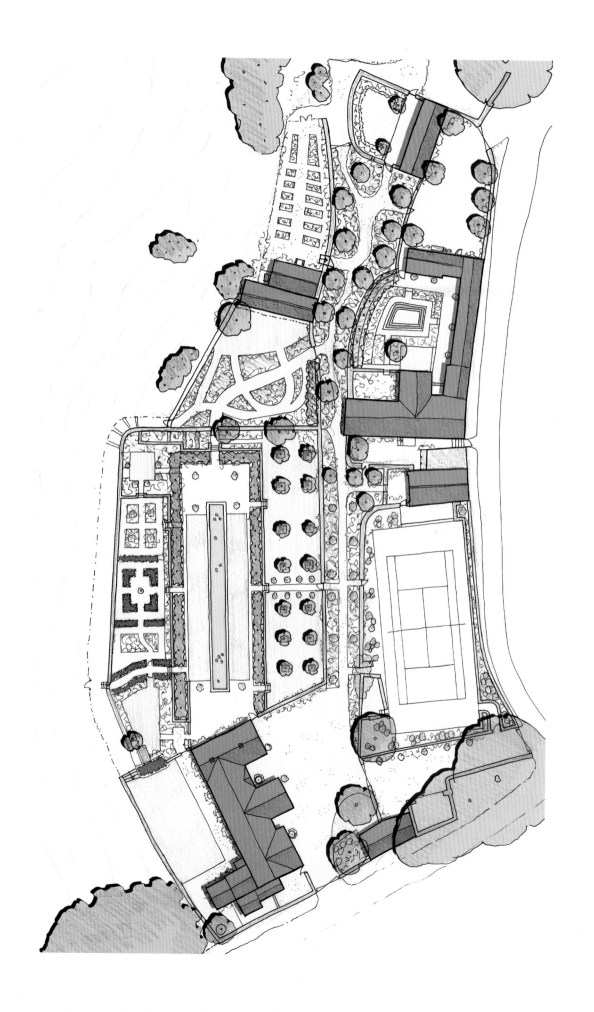

The framework for the gardens at Temple Guiting came together very easily. I created a network of rooms and walks flanked by high drystone walls either protected from or overlooking the ever-changing views. The landscape of the Cotswolds is intimate, so perfectly suited to classical English gardening. The context might be steeped in English history yet the gardens are liberated from it and are a contemporary interpretation. My client's brief was simple. He doesn't like everything dead in winter, he wanted flowers every day and he wanted a 100 foot lily pond … on a hill!

This is a very plant-rich garden. Visitors comment on the tumultuously romantic borders. If one were to study the plan though, it reveals a different story, as the borders are not large yet the spaces are. The soil is thin, stony and dries out fast. The beds have to work hard to give a good display. To stabilize these issues I used a lot of structural planting. If the eye registers green, it immediately amplifies it and I've harnessed this suggestibility throughout the garden. In all areas there is topiary or some form of evergreen.

One of the great natural tricks I learned from the wild French gardens I love is how well some things adapt to growing on stone. Given that this garden is so stony and dry, I thought about all the plants that self-control according to their circumstances. Given that I was making quite formal gardens, they still needed to feel relaxed, or the antiquity of the house could be challenged. I chose a tough group – flag irises, the pretty little daisy erigeron and the usually rampant white valerian – and planted them all around the base of the house. Out of this self-managing ruff grew climbing roses and vines.

The Granary Walk utilizes what was previously the main road through the village, and I altered its mood as it travels through the gardens. It begins close to the house, where it sits between high walls and is made formal by tall columns of yew rhythmically placed through sumptuous borders in pale blues and whites. At the mid-point, against the granary, I placed clipped holm oaks and these mark the change of the planting into something much looser and softer, and it then drifts out another few hundred feet towards the countryside. The central formal garden has tiny flower beds in relation to its size, and here I planted cunning successions or exceptionally strong growers below the hornbeams. So far they have done nothing but flourish.

The Granary Walk becomes riverine as it flows towards the countryside, and the planting becomes looser. Strict topiary gives way to fruit trees still holding the verticality yet in a softer manner (PAGES 210–211).

June in the canal garden captures *Iris* 'Jane Phillips' in its soft light. Although their appearance is brief, they are one of the defining plants of these dry hungry borders (PAGE 212).

It is important to repeat plants through a large garden so, for ease of maintenance as we only have one gardener, I use a lot of roses. *Rosa* x *odorata* 'Pallida' (syn. 'Old Blush'), fronted by box and backed by a venerable beech tree, is England personified (PAGE 213).

The canal becomes both reflecting pool and a wet flower bed of *Nymphaea alba*, the wild white waterlily (OPPOSITE).

My love affair with eryngium species continues unabated (OVERLEAF). The electric blue of *Eryngium alpinum* is a show stopper and the intricate graphics of its ruff are utterly absorbing. Combined with other blues it is a catalyst that unites all the tones of the surrounding flowers, such as *Campanula lactiflora* 'Prichard's Variety', *Salvia* x *superba* and hazy *Geranium* 'Spinners' in a harmonic sequence.

Liberating

It takes at least a calendar year to design a garden well. Steady progress in any subject makes it an enjoyable experience. Landscaping is unquestionably built for comfort and not for speed. The *steady pulse of the seasons is the rhythm of life to a garden*. The process of building draws to a conclusion and at last the embryonic idea is seen in all its glorious dimensions. The garden is born. And this is where we let it go and watch it draw its first full breath of life.

When it is all over, it can begin

Thinking about a new place takes time. Absorbing its characteristics and getting to know the people can't be rushed. It can be hard to justify what can feel like a long, long wait while you cogitate. Time is needed to manage all the detailed processes and statutory permissions to get the design to a point where building can begin. Building a garden takes longer. Even if everyone wishes to work at speed, it just can't be rushed. All the vagaries of the natural world intercede and remind us that our puny human willpower is no match for the steady turning of the Earth and the complexity of seasons and weather systems. Several more years might easily slip by in the process of building and planting the garden. I enjoy the reminder this work gives me, that we are just a tiny part of a gargantuan planet patiently orbiting through space. Every day brings a new poetry of weather. The very earth itself is mutable and this inconstancy affects the process of building. I'm referring to mud. Mud is a dominant opponent in building, and sanguine landscapers understand that it has to be respected or it will haunt them.

Plants need to be found and grown for the projects, and even in the most high-tech nurseries the growth is still occurring at a natural pace dictated by the plant species and the seasons. I can often, but not always, accelerate the visual maturity of a garden by buying large specimens of topiary and trees, yet even the biggest of these is still an infant in tree terms.

Patience is most definitely a virtue in landscaping and it is rewarded by beauty that will outlast most of us. Making gardens well means leaving a legacy far in excess of our own short lifespan, and for me that is the attraction of this art form. The point at which the completed garden is handed over is the moment that it begins to fly. From this moment on the quality of thinking that went into its creation is tested. My fundamental feeling is that it is the structure of the garden — its walls, surfaces, routes, views, water, structural planting such as trees and shrubbery, topiary and hedges — that ultimately counts. Herbaceous planting, however exquisite, is evanescent. Flowers are not what make a garden last but what

This simple border has persevered now for fifteen years with a pared-back mix of salvias, *Elaeagnus* 'Quicksilver' and *Rosa* x *odorata* 'Mutabilis', punctuated by *Stipa gigantea* (BELOW). It doesn't have to be complicated to work.

Gardening is all about change and the moments of perfection are fleeting and personal. The salvias and alliums are turning to seed while the verbena and roses are just emerging (OPPOSITE). The gardener handles the mercury of gardening with sensitivity and skill.

Creating an all-glass building in an inner city is a bold move (PREVIOUS PAGES). I embedded it in planting that undulates through the seasons.

Gardening from scratch, as I do, it is hard to convey to others what's in my mind's eye. About five years after the garden is completed, something mysterious happens. As if by magic the whole garden settles. Planting balances, materials have aged and the whole picture becomes clear.

I try to make a relationship in the design of the garden planting to what is happening on the horizon. Flowing the garden mellifluously out into its surroundings makes everything gentle on the eye (OPPOSITE).

The water plants are texturally similar to plants in the adjacent bed (ABOVE). As everything grows and blends together, there will be no visual jarring.

attract in the short term. I am accepting of the fact that herbaceous planting might only last for a few years in the incarnation I create and will change and metamorphose depending on who is caring for it. That is one of the mercurial pleasures of gardening. I enjoy making the spaces, the flower beds, knowing that they will alter as time goes on, within the bigger structure of the garden. What I really love is the maturing structure. Returning to gardens I made early in my career, there is a sobering thrill in seeing trees grown up and walls and ironwork patinated with lichens and mosses, as though they have always stood there. There is no sense of achievement like it. To have engendered something that lives on, developing its own character, shaped by the inhabitants, environment and the climate, is a marvellous feeling.

Conservation

Hold reverence for the earth and the whole natural system of which we are part

It is an underpinning philosophy of my work to make landscapes that are self-supporting and appropriate to their location. It seems ill mannered to inflict something on the earth that it might reject like a baby spitting out food. The earth does rebuff things it doesn't like, so this is borne in mind when designing. The way world economics functions these days present many paradoxes to the process of working complicity with the earth, but overall we do what we can. As we operate in a global economy inevitably some things we want come from abroad. I'm accepting of that on the basis that if the better plants were grown overseas then I'd rather have them even if it means freight costs. On most of the projects, wherever they may be, we look at using species of plants compatible to the native soil, locally found hard landscape materials, closed water systems and, if we are influencing the architecture, we use as much self-generated heating as possible.

A wild brown trout stream flows swiftly over Oxfordshire gravel. Initially we didn't realize we had a river, as everything was so overgrown (BELOW). The discovery and subsequent restoration of the stream were highs in what was already an incredible project.

Under the sheltering canopy of an incredibly ancient ivy arch is where *Eryngium giganteum*, Miss Willmott's ghost, has taken up residence (OPPOSITE). As gardens mature, the plants make their own decisions about their pleasure.

My garden is fully mature now and teetering on the brink of a renaissance (OVERLEAF). The hefty vines sitting in their pots are a sure sign that I've run out of room and yet my desire for new planting continues unabated. What next?

Since I was very young I've been aware of water scarcity. We used to spend summers in the south of France at my family's vineyards. It was blissfully baking hot. The only water at home came from a tower well in the garden and we used to winch it up twice a day. The water was chalk white from the limy rocky aquifer and only used for washing bodies and washing up. After washing we had to carry the buckets of used water to the vegetable garden and water the plants at dusk. Never were we allowed to water in the hard sun of the day, as it just evaporated and was useless. Bear in mind this was only thirty-odd years ago and it was a smart house – it was just a fact that water was scarce and treated with respect. For drinking water my uncle drove once a week up into the mountains about forty miles away. He would load vast glass flagons into the back of the car. They fitted tightly in their protective woven rattan baskets. We would head up to Le Soulié, a tiny hamlet in the Montagnes Noires. Here, gushing from a well mouth, there was a clear cold freshwater spring. It was an underground river whose water was free for all-comers. We would wait in the cool shade as he filled the flasks. This was the drinking and cooking water for the week. In that climate it was like drinking liquid diamonds – chilled, precious and delicious. He would bang the huge corks into the flagons with a small wooden mallet and

These houses and gardens at home in France have blended seamlessly into their wild riverside situation (ABOVE). It is my dream to make gardens that are completely comfortable in their setting and where nothing jars the eye or defiles nature.

This thriving wilderness garden is unwatered by anything other than rain (OPPOSITE). It has survived beautifully for years this way and the unusual mix of planting is well suited to both the ethos and the conditions.

we would return home slowly down the precipitous mountain roads with the great weight of water apparent in the creaking suspension. I have never taken water for granted since. In our gardens we try to save water where we can, and my love of dams, natural ponds and water bodies is far greater than my interest in water used for fountains or features. Researching historic water courses or reading a landscape to find them is a very sound idea. I've used water diviners very successfully before now to find old wells, springs and aquifers. Springs, streams and rivers must be maintained and cared for. Water supports life and is, therefore, essential to any plan.

On many small estates there are pockets of woodland and copses. There seems to be a prevailing idea these days that being 'sustainable' means not husbanding woodland but I'm not in that camp. It is good for the health of relic woodland, indeed of any woodland, to be worked. If we ever inherit any on a project, we try to find a woodman to care for it. Coppicing and clearing provides firewood and useable material such as beanpoles and pea sticks for the vegetable garden. On a few projects we have incorporated woodchip boilers to provide heat for the house and swimming pool. It's an investment to do this properly and we are quite good at designing small industrial estates to accommodate all the drying sheds and machinery required for this. It's not really gardening but it is certainly part of creating a self-sufficient system!

Apart from wood and water as the fundamentals of conservation, the next in the hierarchy is the hedge – I have already laid out their undeniable benefits (see pages 206–7). They have so much seasonal beauty with flowers, catkins, fruit and autumn colour. They are a must for every garden.

I really do believe that the meek will inherit the Earth, as they are the people who still use it to live from in a modest and direct way. Evolving to supermarkets, central heating and cash machines leaves us in a much more precarious position.

This green lane of box and espaliered pears leads to a quiet corner by the apple trees where I hid a swing in a tiny glade (BELOW AND OPPOSITE). Gardens need pockets of seclusion and privacy for peaceful thought. So much in our lives is over-attended to that perhaps gardens are the last refuge of undisturbed peace.

The art of gardening
Handing over the reins

Now that the garden is built and planted, it is time to introduce the gardener. I recently encouraged a well-known garden magazine to feature a young professional gardener every month. Without a constant supply of new gardening talent we designers might as well hang up our pencils. The ultimate success of a scheme lies in their hands. Gardening used to be a skill apparent in almost every family, as so many people grew their own food and gardened, and as much an oral and practical tradition as a competently taught one. There were good training programmes in dedicated horticultural colleges, and horticulture was an accepted employment route. After a worrying decline in interest I believe that this downward trend is now changing for the better. There is a resurgence of awareness in the multifaceted skill base required to be a gardener. It is a skill that requires innate talent and an affinity with the natural world, combined with a character that enjoys solitude and detail.

Every variety of plant has a personality that wants understanding. Considering the needs of an unnaturally integrated group of species brought together by design is a challenging skill. In my new garden I have inherited some rather good flower beds and am studying them for a year before I decide how to manipulate them to suit me, or whether to keep them at all. I feel a need to honour the many hours of thought, love and care invested by the departing gardener. The gardens were planned carefully by her and are beautifully balanced. She was a watercolourist and designed them to create great washes of colour in softly varied mounds that she could then paint. The colour choices are poised and thoughtful across a spectrum from palest china pink to rich deep magenta. These arrangements are beautiful in early spring as their leaves emerge in varied shapes and tints of green, with sheets of tulips running through them. As they grow, the mid-summer explosion of flower covers the dying and drying tulip stems. So far so good! By late summer, however, the roses are fading and the geraniums are growing tired. Their leaves are desiccating, the flowers more intermittent. There is nothing of significant interest left to underpin them. Drastic action must be taken to cut them all back and allow a fresh leaf flush in autumn. I feel a bit bereft, as there won't be much happening between late summer and Christmas. This is clearly a spring and summer garden. I prefer the gentler experience of

Having been consumed by the creation of the garden, I continue the story with my successor, the gardener. Between us, with help from nature, we nurture the future. — VITRUVIUS

The eternal flower bed flows steadily on through the seasons outside the kitchen window (OPPOSITE). It is made almost exclusively from tall narrow plants that camouflage each other as they progress through flowering and decline.

Quiet space, even in a relatively small garden, is useful. I've a patch of long grass studded with wildflowers occupying about a quarter of the garden (ABOVE). It amplifies what happens elsewhere and is soothing to look at.

Everyone loves arches. I've been trying to take them out and many voices rise in protest against this act of Philistinism (OVERLEAF). Perhaps they are right. I shall persevere! Strange coloured parma violet blooms of *Rosa* 'Veilchenblau' generate an equally strange mood in me. I'm not sure it's my colour, yet I keep it for the unsettling effect it has on me.

interesting things appearing and disappearing throughout the year – sparks and lilts of floral interest held together with good bones of topiary or purposeful shrubs. This abstract description of planting cadences is all very well, but it is in the mind's eye of the creator and about as personal as choosing clothes, so how does it get communicated to a gardener? How can they be informed and inspired and then liberated to develop the scheme?

I like to get the gardener involved during the build. The skill sets for landscaping and gardening are very different, and the finesse that a gardener brings is needed almost as soon as the garden is formed. While a landscaper arranges the structure of the garden's design and fills in the beds with soil, it is the gardener who takes on the enriching and nurturing of the soil. Once the planting is done, it is the gardener who waters and weeds and tends the plants. In any new garden I say it takes three to five years for the species to begin balancing out. This takes a lot of explaining to the new owners. This is where the designer and gardener are collaborators who stabilize the expectations of the owner and take them on the enjoyable journey of the maturing garden.

The patient protector
Collaboration and care

Ideas always need practical skills to back them up. Roses I always plant in autumn, having first brutalized them with severe root pruning and top pruning. I was taught to do this by Brian Wray, the gardener who looked after one of the first gardens I ever built. Brian was retired when I met him and he agreed to garden for me, as I had built the garden in an old walled garden to a stately home where his father had been the Victorian Head Gardener. 'I know every nail in these walls,' said Brian. 'Father had me in here with him a lot of the time.' Brian was a great teacher, as gardening ran pure and swift through his veins. Rash acts, he taught me, are seldom helpful. A limb cut from a tree without forethought can never be replaced. Poor pruning can result in deformity or disease or loss of life. Soil is the root of health. We devoted a lot of time to soil and as a result I always design huge composting bays in my jobs. Pruning is something I fear and revere. My uncle, whose livelihood depended on good pruning in his vineyards, taught me how and also instilled such fear of making mistakes in me that I have never overcome this timidity, even with Brian's patient guidance. Clean, precise and beautiful pruning is one of the greatest skills a gardener can possess. Predicting the ultimate shape of a tree, or the flowering of a rose, or fruiting of a vine is an art. Maybe if one grows up pruning, it might seem self-evident, but few of us do. Much like drystone walling is either your gift or not, so I believe is pruning.

So the gradual handover of the design to the gardener is a satisfying process. My projects live on happily in their care. Kevin Walker has cared for one of my London gardens now for many years now, and my heart sang when I saw it again to photograph it for this book. Kevin had digested all our initial discussions on its evolution and my clients had instructed him to carry out my vision on their behalf. As a result, the garden has grown into its skin and looks settled and beautiful. This is the joy of gardening. Collaboration and care.

The regular care of this tender *Rosa laevigata* by Carl Jones, the gardener, results in a magnificent wall of blooms (OPPOSITE). His knowledge and foresight are channelled through his clean sharp secateurs. Gardeners work alone and yet their skills are on display and admired by all who see the beauty of their efforts.

Marcus Aurelius urged us to remember when we arise in the morning to think of what a precious privilege it is to be alive – to breathe, to think, to enjoy, to love. And I would add to garden. The patient love and care that goes into a garden is a gift for life.

Beauty is essential
Health and strength

Gardening is good for you. It is an irrefutable fact. Physical exercise in the fresh air is good for the body. Tending for something other than us, nurturing and encouraging life, is good for a sense of wellbeing and purpose. We live in very egocentric times and it is quite difficult to find activities that are engrossing and help take us out of ourselves. The way we live and work seems to create the stress that causes so much unhappiness. Having your labours rewarded with flowers, fruit and vegetables is an obvious benefit of gardening. Proudly sharing home-grown food with friends and decorating the house with flowers we cultivate and pick ourselves is a source of quiet joy. All of these things make for a better life. I believe that through my own turbulent upbringing it was my chosen daily interaction with nature that kept me growing straight and true. As an adult I gardened for my own sense of constancy and peace. Wherever I've lived I've always needed access to a small patch of earth. When I worked in mental health in a deprived part of a big city, it was clear to see the benefit that it brought my troubled clients. I have continued to make strong links between health and gardening throughout my twin careers.

The health benefit of gardening is very much in the *Zeitgeist*. I am proud to see it appearing in governmental papers on health and being promoted in schools and institutions. I believe that this is due in no small part to some primal fear we share now that we are so dislocated from the Earth we walk on. We are living in an epoch where we are very aware of our species' fragility. For the first time in human history we are liberated from the backbreaking toil of working the land to feed ourselves. We rely on the global agricultural superstructure to do it for us. With this liberation comes anxiety – humans are designed to feed and clothe themselves. We feel a justifiable unease at our lack of self-sufficiency. Working in some of the far-flung places I've been to, I am reminded that there are people who are still genuinely able to support themselves, albeit it is now regarded as subsistence living. Even in these impoverished environments I still found gardens that were there just for their beauty. It seems that beauty is profoundly necessary to wellbeing. Many people, more able and academically equipped than me, have seized on this subject and written excellent books, so I shan't overegg it here. Suffice to say – find a patch of the earth to call your own and set to work. It will transform your life from the inside out and for the better.

The sketch shows that the atrium courtyard I designed for Chelsea and Westminster Hospital allows trees to grow up to full height (ABOVE). It is a multilevel open-plan space, and many wards of sick people share the view to the plants. Nature in this context is magnetically appealing. In a predominantly white interior the warm colours and hand-crafted materials are almost alien. I chose colours akin to sunshine and used art by Albrecht Dürer to humanize the huge bespoke planters (OPPOSITE). The planting is lush and obligingly vigorous. The garden is used therapeutically within the hospital.

Down to earth
Our garden heritage

The seed heads of the pasqueflower, *Pulsatilla vulgaris*, are as beautiful as the flower (OPPOSITE). They are tender and tenacious at the same time. They blow away, get trapped in rocky crevices and delight a Spartan landscape in spring with their rich velvety flowers.

The pergola was a priority in this garden and I very much appreciate having made it now (ABOVE). The roses are fully grown and beautifully tended over the hand-crafted iron strap work, and the oak has weathered down to silvery grey. The children that ran through it years ago are now grown, and it bears witness to the transformations in family life.

A garden becomes an heirloom. When I was small we visited, as families do, many gardens that were open to the public as well as private ones. Repetition in garden visiting is a good thing, as they bear recurrent viewing, and the temperament of the place, the period in which it was made and the personality of the maker soon become apparent. Hidcote was the great case in point and we visited every season in turn, my mother, aunt and I. The garden felt familiar, and although Lawrence Johnston was obviously a wealthy man, the garden spoke of things other than his money. He was clearly passionate about plants and shared friendships with other plant lovers, such as Norah Lyndsay, as gardeners do. He had travelled a great deal and his time in South Africa had seeped into his planting palette, giving it a varied vocabulary. The Cotswolds always had a feel of France for me, because of the similarities in the limestone, I think, and it was unsurprising to discover that Johnston had also made a garden in France. So from my earliest recollections I knew that gardens were a vital part of our cultural heritage.

Over time I became more and more engrossed in how the structure of a garden made me feel. To this day I can't bear Versailles. The exaggerated grandeur and the greatly over-scaled vistas and rides weary me and make me ache for something gentler. Versailles feels to me like an ego out of control, like a world about to collapse, a power that is about to fail – overstretched and straining in its will to dominate. I felt self-conscious that I couldn't relate to it. I don't like feeling stupid in a landscape!

Very gradually it dawned on me that the environment we create to live in can affect our sense of self quite potently. This was ultimately what made me want to create landscapes and gardens for people. I wanted to make benign, handsome, complicit environments where the intimate experiences of our personal lives can be enjoyed. I want very much to find the true note of a garden so that it can live long and benefit the people who use it. Recently it gave me great pleasure to make an earthwork in one of our landscapes. The artist Paul Nash's wonderful Wittenham Clumps paintings, the original landscape of which is near to our site, inspired it. I created a miniature stylized version and planted it with oak trees. My client's children are small and we love the idea that by the time they are ready to marry they could do so in the little circular grove of oaks. The house will get passed through the family line so we already know that this garden is for them and the generations beyond them. For me this is the greatest satisfaction, knowing that the gardens will have stories and personal histories made in them.

My mother gardened, or tried to. Her children and their phalanxes of herbivorous pets thwarted her best efforts. From her I learned a great deal about plants and send her my retrospective sympathy, as our advancing furry army steadily demolished all her beautiful borders. She instilled in me that gardening is a vital part of life and she surprised us all by becoming, out of nowhere, a remarkably good vegetable gardener in her middle years. Surprising as until then she had been an impossibly glamorous young French woman enveloped in a cloud of Guerlain with perfect hair and make-up. So much life took place in the garden when we were kids and these days my own is filled with activity. Parties and lunches and village open days complement the daily routines of watering, weeding and deadheading. We eat out there, have early morning cups of tea, the garden dacha is home to photo shoots and comedy show rehearsals and drumming. When family come to stay, it is transformed into the imaginative landscapes of five-year-olds: storm-tossed seas, lighthouses, nests of dragons and gremlins. The cat operates his own timetable and litters the back doorstep with corpses.

This sense of the garden's heirloom quality is brought sharply home to me now, as recently my mother died. During her short illness her main anxiety was for the future of her garden and her fear for its neglect. She was sanguine about her old age and her inevitable departure – it comes to us all. I promised her I would look after it – after all, we had gardened together in it for the last twenty years whenever I was with her in France, so it was natural that I would. Her friends and I would dig and weed and laugh and drink with her, and both she and the garden are well known and loved. Her relief was palpable and touching. Gardening brings the best out in people, I find, and softens even the most intractable character. The practicalities of gardening from a thousand miles away were soon solved, as I unearthed a great gardener, Jean Dubois, living in the hills nearby. Together we have renovated the garden, and Monsieur Cabot fixed the little chateau in it that she loved. Jean and I now enjoy our enthusiastic plant-orientated friendship, looking after the garden between us by email, augmented by my intermittent visits. His mother has moved in next door to the garden so that cements the relationship further. The garden is on view to the village so it is important that it is loved, as my mother was, and tended, as it should be. Gardens are created to be handed on. An heirloom, a long evolving story. That is a garden:

Tree planting is a natural baton race. The constant succession from seed to sapling to tree is managed by the vagaries of nature and only the strong survive.

The magnificent old oak dominates this image and yet, there behind him is part of the long avenue we just planted using huge nursery trees of *Tilia cordata* nearly 7m (23 feet) tall (OPPOSITE). Musing on the future appearance of this scene is a source of deep pleasure.

An emancipated landscape
free to roam

INVERNESS-SHIRE, SCOTLAND

––––––––––

The nature of the project presented itself to me completely.
It first needed a horticultural defibrillator to shock it
back to life. It needed protection to restore a natural and
legitimate seed bank. Grazing pressure had to be removed,
allowing the land to heal itself and recover its strength.

In dark grey are depicted the vestiges of the original estate buildings, and the new lodge is visible in pale grey. In the vastness of this estate the dwellings are clustered together and are wrapped all around in beech trees, now maturing and reaching the end of their brief Highland lives. Providing a succession plantation and the possibility of a naturally regenerating seed bank was the central thrust of the design. Beauty occurs naturally in this landscape, and just needed a positive boost and a reversion from the hand of man.

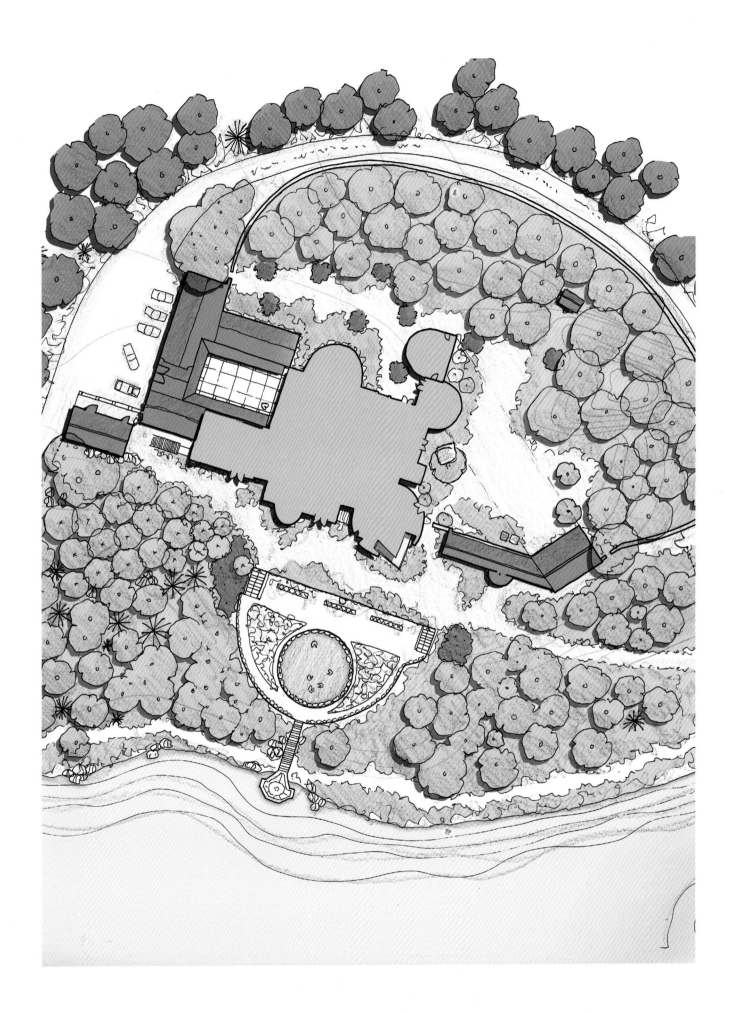

Just after dawn I stepped out of the sleeper train from London onto a tiny deserted platform. Some hours later I saw a speck of a Land Rover coming towards me. The Highlands of Scotland make one feel small. It is a wild magnificent place that neither deserves nor requires taming.

The project centred on finding a suitable landscape language for the newly designed lodge, which was under construction by the Toronto-based architect Moshe Safdie. The lodge is alien and owes nothing to its Highland home set in 68,000 acres, of which I took over a couple of hundred for the project.

The landscaping was informed by the past, both the past successes and mistakes. The estate had come into being at the height of Victorian plant-hunting mania. The original owner, Sir John Stirling-Maxwell, had intelligently exploited the natural characteristics of this cool high wet place

by trialling foreign tree species. He planted Sitka spruce, which relished the thin acidic soil and constant soft rain. Worryingly, they had been so successful they were now endangering all else.

I had a good gut feeling for what I was in for. High rainfall: we had 364 consecutive days of rain during the build. Thin acidic glacial moraine with a skim of something that could hardly be considered soil, more like rotted moss and dander from the reddish *Molinia* that covers the ground. The rampant Sitka spruce plantations had become non-viable for the forestry commission and were in senescence, gradually starving light and life from the hill streams and, ultimately, the loch as they grew old and died.

An already delicate ecosystem was stressed and exhausted by overgrazing. This was a dying landscape. I was optimistic though. The reversal works incredibly fast and I stopped my ears to the

negativists who assured me nothing would ever grow. Erecting mile upon mile of deer fencing stopped grazing. The miracle of regeneration was instantaneous. To augment it we planted thousands of baby trees – birch, rowan, alder and pine, all indigenous. They took off like rockets.

Beside the lodge I wanted to create a 'relic' garden using herbaceous plants from Sir John's archives. His original plans were for a highly structured Victorian garden, now long defunct bar a few obvious elements such as a lovely rockery and a circular pool, which would be inappropriate to restore in its totality. I restored the pool and rockery then naturalized plants such as panther lily, lupins, ferns, campanulas and Himalayan cowslip from Sir John's lists. Reading the geology of the terrain and the near history of the site gave me the necessary tools to create an arrangement that will last far longer than I will.

Sir John Stirling-Maxwell's original garden was painstakingly uncovered, almost like an archaeological dig, every stone lifted and reset and then allowed to relax back into Highland life (PAGE 250). The restored mirror pool is still as the original Victorian owner intended, focusing the eye for a moment before it travels the 5 miles of the loch and across to Ben Nevis in the mists (OPPOSITE).

The sauna blends seamlessly into its gently cleared grove of trees and naturalized *Rhododendron luteam*. No ornamentation is needed (PAGE 251).

October is the month that the landscape comes alive with the incredible fiery tints of autumn softened by the ceaseless misting rain. I can almost feel Sir John's feet on the steps as he made his daily round of his treasured plants (ABOVE). The deadly mass of stultifying Sitka spruce still seen further around the loch contrasts with the effect of clearance: deciduous trees with their mast and fallen leaf returning life to the loch (PAGES 248–249).

Moshe Safdie's magnificent contemporary lodge rises curiously from the now-mature plantation of the original house. Emanating from this point is a pure and natural seed bank that might one day repopulate the deer-grazed hills with rowan, birch and pine (PAGES 254–56).

Acknowledgements

I had no idea what goes into making a book!

To my patrons, past, present and future I offer my unreserved and heartfelt thanks for inviting me to do what I love doing most for you. To those of you who have been generous enough to let me share the result of our collaborations in the book, I can't thank you enough.

My heartfelt thanks go to:
Jacqui Small – every carefully chosen word and raised eyebrow counts! Thank you for your trust.
Sian Parkhouse – for her kindness and forbearance, intelligence, lucid light touch and precision editing.
Eszter Karpati – for her calm and her humour.
Emma Heyworth-Dunn – for keeping it all going.
Mark Paton of Here Design – a lucky conversation 6,000 feet above sea level on the equator resulted in this book being so beautiful.
Fiona Lindsay – my patient agent at Limelight Celebrity Management for her unstinting years of support waiting for me to produce something.

To Todd Longstaffe-Gowan and Tom Stuart-Smith, my old muckers.

My studio associates:
Maude Pinet, Živilé Mačiukaité, Anna Cassavetti, Tinyue Liu, Pernille Bisgaard Jensen, Chris Page, Janet Paterson and the indefatigable 'author's sidekick' Laura Diggens. To Jared Lockhart for the early years. I salute you all – you made/make every day a pleasure.

Andrew Montgomery for the superb photography commissioned for the book and his gracious acceptance of sharing the pages with the past.

To the exceptional skills of the very best of photographers who, over the last sixteen years, have so outstandingly, and generously, recorded my work. Thank you.
Charlie Hopkinson
Andrew Lawson
Jason Ingram
Allan Pollok-Morris
Nicola Browne
Nadia MacKenzie
Tom Mannion
Annie Schlechter
Marianne Majerus

To Robert Crocker. Your presence here needs no explanation.
To Ptolemy Dean, dear friend, collaborator and father of my magnificent godchild, Octavia.
To Maureen Doherty. Constant source of wisdom.
To Mark Straver. Ma insisted.
To my fellow Brothers at the Art Workers' Guild.
To Paula, Piet, Brian, Skye and Victoria for our friendships and your understanding of my work.

PHOTOGRAPHY CREDITS
Andrew Montgomery (Copyright © Jacqui Small LLP and Jinny Blom)
Pages 4, 6, 11, 14–15, 17, 19, 22–23, 25, 26, 27, 28, 29, 31, 33, 34, 35, 38–39, 40, 41, 44, 45, 46–47, 52, 54, 55, 60, 61, 63 top & bottom, 64, 65, 66, 67, 70, 71, 74, 75, 76 top left, 83, 86 bottom, 87 bottom, 90, 91 top & bottom, 94, 95, 97 top & bottom, 102–103, 104, 108–109, 112–13, 114, 115, 117 top & bottom, 118–19, 120, 121, 122–23, 124, 125, 126, 127, 136 top, 140–41, 142, 143, 144, 145 top & bottom, 146, 147, 150–51, 152, 153, 154–55, 157 top, 161, 166 top, 165, 167, 171, 172–73, 175, 176–77, 178, 184, 186–87, 188, 190 top left & top right, 191, 193 all, 194–95, 197 bottom, 198, 201, 202–203, 204, 205, 210–11, 213, 214, 216, 217, 222, 223, 224, 225, 227, 228–29, p230, 231, 236, 237, 243, 248–49, 250, 251, 252, 253

Charlie Hopkinson
Pages 1, 50–51, 53, 56–57, 58, 68–69, 73 top & bottom, 76 top right, bottom left & bottom right, 77, 80 top & bottom, 82, 86 top, 87 top, 89, 92–93, 105, 106 top & bottom, 116, 128 top & bottom, 129 all, 136 bottom, 157 bottom, 160, 162 top, 163, 164 top & bottom, 166 bottom, 170, 174, 180, 181, 182, 183, 185 bottom, 190 bottom, 196, 197 top, 220–21, 226, 234, 235, 239, 241, 242, 245

Nicola Browne
Pages 43, 78, 79, 85, 96, 199, 200, 206, 232, 233

Andrew Lawson
Pages 9, 18, 159, 179, 189, 207, 212

Tom Mannion
Pages 130 top, 131, 137, 162 bottom

Annie Schlechter
Pages 30, 81, 168, 169

Jason Ingram
Pages 2–3, 98–99, 156

Allan Pollok-Morris
Page 84, 133 left, 185 top, 254–55

Nadia MacKenzie
Pages 132, 133 right

Marianne Majerus
Pages 134–5

Jinny Blom
Page 130 bottom

Artworks
Jinny Blom pages 31, 37, 55, 62, 72, 81, 88, 101, 139, 158, 192, 197, 209, 240, 247
Pernille Bisgaard Jensen page 59

Map page 32 is a detail of CCC Archives Maps 68, copyright © and by permission of The President and Fellows of Corpus Christi College, Oxford